Dick Wolfsie's New Book

longer

funnier

cheaper

Author's note:

Nobody could remember the name of my last book. People just walked into bookstores and said "Do you have Dick Wolfsie's new book?"

I'm hoping this will make things easier.

ISBN

Cover design: Cherrie LiFonti
Book design: Karen Kennedy
Proofreading and copyediting: J. Heidi Newman

Printed and bound in the United States of America

Publisher's note: Many of the pieces in this book were originally published as weekly newspaper columns throughout the state of Indiana.

Additional copies of *Dick Wolfsie's New Book* can be purchased at most Marsh Supermarkets or by sending $12.95 to Queen City Press, 9801 Fall Creek Road, Indianapolis, IN 46256. Dick can be reached at Wolfsie@aol.com.

Contents

Foreword
By Brett Wolfsie (Dick's son)

You can watch my dad on Channel 8's *Daybreak* every morning. You can read his weekly syndicated humor column in one of 15 newspapers, listen to him on the radio, or read one of three books he has written. If we could just get my dad his own billboard, he could annoy people five different ways.

Afterword
(in case you never get to the back of the book)

And look for Dick Wolfsie's new book, (not *Dick Wolfsie's New Book*), *Indiana Curiosities*. Published by Globe-Pequot Press, it's chock full of all the fascinating people and places that Dick has visited over the years, plus many new ones he's turned up just for this book.

Check your bookstores in the spring of 2003 for *Indiana Curiosities*.

Introduction

This is my New Book.
New Book, say hello to:

_____
(fill in your name here)

Dick Wolfsie's New Book

longer ◎ funnier ◎ cheaper

Brilliant
Observations
About Life*

* In my opinion

Work Detail

Last week I attended a party and people were going around the table lamenting about their obsessive-compulsive idiosyncrasies. I was astounded to hear what people consider to be neurotic, rather than just normal, everyday attention to detail.

One guy claimed that he arranged all the hangers in his closet so that the shirts went in the same direction, then he buttoned each top button and then grouped the shirts by color from darkest to lightest. Incredibly, there were people at the table who laughed at this.

A lady, somewhat embarrassed, admitted to making two "to do" lists every night—one arranged geographically, and one in order of importance. People were shaking their heads and snickering. I don't blame them. Where's the alphabetical list?

Another guy, who admitted he was in therapy, said he polishes all his shoes every night, waxes the shoe trees and arranges the shoes in his closet in order of the date he bought them. So why's he in therapy?

One woman, who seemed reluctant to speak, finally confessed that she not only separates laundry by white and color, but that she does a red load, a blue load, a green load, and a yellow load. This I did find astounding. I mean, any idiot knows you can't wash royal and navy blue together.

One older gentleman said he can't go to work each day unless the garage has been swept and all the tools have been put away in their proper place. Okay, am I missing something here? Did this guy actually go to bed with the garage a mess?

A very attractive young lady explained to the group that when she pays bills out of her checkbook, she uses a different color pen for each type of purchase. Groceries are in blue ink, clothing is in black ink, and utilities are in red. Now, you show me a person who only uses three different color pens and I'll show you a guy who's not keeping track of his entertainment expenses.

One guy broke into tears after admitting that he vacuumed his car out every night when he got home from work and that if he missed even one cleaning, he lost all feelings of intimacy for his wife. Okay, now this really is nuts. Even I can see that. A normal man should be able to go almost a week without vacuuming the SUV and still feel romantic.

One lady told the group that she spends about four hours cleaning the house before the maids come and then another three hours cleaning after they leave. Wow, three hours' additional cleaning after they leave? I'd sure love to find a maid service that good.

And finally, one lady admitted that all the spices in her spice rack were arranged alphabetically, but that lately she was experiencing some serious trauma deciding if garlic salt should be shelved under the S or the G. I told her that in my cupboard, I put virgin olive oil under V, but that I bought another bottle that I put under O, just in case. I love helping people. I should have been a shrink.

When the conversation got around to me, I was a little reluctant to share my personal quirks. Plus, when it was my turn to talk, I hadn't finished polishing the silverware. I wanted to get it done before the bus boy cleared the table.

Garage...
Door Openers

I like to putter around the garage. I used to think that this was a sign of getting older, but I'm more convinced than ever that great things happen in garages. If you haven't started puttering, it's not too late.

Bill Gates, it is said, started Microsoft in his garage. And the people who syndicate the Oprah Winfrey show started their concept in a garage. I have a good friend, right here in Indy, who started his multi-million-dollar candy business in his tiny garage.

This has really begun to bug me. I have never started anything in my garage. Well, I did start my 1978 Ford Pinto when it was only 35 degrees outside. I should get some points for that. And let's see, I did start to clean the garage once. I never finished, so I can't take credit there.

Of course, when you realize how many creative ideas originated in people's garages and how much money has been generated from them, you wonder why parents still push the Wharton School of Business.

I mean, the cost of college tuition now exceeds $100,000 for four years. You can get a really decent garage for about a third of that and have it the rest of your life. I spent a total of seven years in college and never had an idea that was worth more than a couple of bucks. My mistake? Living in the dorm, of course.

What kills me is how many times my very own father said to me, "Sure, you can come home and live after college, but you'll have to stay in the garage." I never really appreciated my father's wisdom until now.

I don't know what it is about garages. I have no recollection of reading about anyone who ever made an important discovery in his living room. And when's the last time someone said to you, "You know, I just had the greatest idea while up in my attic"? And spare bedrooms? I don't think one earth-shattering accomplishment has ever been generated from a spare bedroom.

Even criminals love garages. You hear all the time how a terrorist built a bomb in his garage. But when's the last time that a killer planned his next murder in the sunroom? Or a bank robber charted his Brinks robbery on the screened-in porch? Garages just bring out the best in people.

Maybe it's the fumes. In my garage you get that wonderful mixture of gasoline, bug spray and paint. Those chemical reactions go right to your brain and could result in a five-state killing spree or Oprah Winfrey on TV in 240 cities. Don't underestimate the power of a garage.

I sat in my garage the other day—just sat there reflecting on all the time I've wasted at the beach contemplating Plato or in my bedroom listening to Mozart. And for what? So some computer geek could sit in the corner of his garage straddling a lawnmower and make 90 billion dollars?

"Billy Gates, what are you doing out there in the garage?"

"Sitting out here has given me an idea that could make us rich, Mom. We'll take all this junk in the garage and sell it right on our driveway. People in the neighborhood will come buy stuff that we were going to throw out. We'll call it a garage sale."

"You're a genius, Billy. Any other bright ideas?"

"How about a personal computer that almost everyone can afford and I'll put an operating system in it that will so monopolize the industry that I'll be rich."

"Billy?"

"Yes, Mom?"

"You better get out of the garage. Those fumes are getting to you."

So, if you like to putter around your garage, do it with your head held high. Just don't trip over the snowblower.

Aering Grievances

The men who live in my cul-de-sac aerate their lawns. I'm going to give you their real names: Jeff, Mark and Norm. I'm telling you this because there's a good chance that because of this unnecessary demonstration of virility, I may put my house up for sale and I'd feel guilty if a faithful reader like yourself ended up in the same neighborhood.

I discovered this aeration situation the other day when my wife and I arrived home from a Sunday brunch and saw Jeff wrestling with what appeared to be a 200-horsepower lawn machine. The really strange part was that Jeff was not aerating his own lawn, but Norm's lawn—an apparent act of great selflessness, unless you take into account that he had simply lost control of the behemoth and was desperately trying to steer the machine back to his own front yard. Then Mark, watching Jeff from his living room window, had come outside to request that he be given a chance to aerate. Norm also wanted in. This scam was so ingenious that it made Tom Sawyer look like an amateur.

I have never aerated my lawn. In fact, I don't think I've ever said or written the word "aerated" before. If it weren't for spell-check on my computer, the first line of this story would have been: "The men who live in my cul-de-sac airrate their lawns." I think that once I accidentally went from liquefy to aerate while making a strawberry shake in my wife's blender. That's the extent of my experience.

Now that I know what aerating is, I'm pretty sure I want no part of it. Here are some of the things I'd rather do than aerate my lawn:

1. *Clean the gutters with my own toothbrush*
2. *Tar the driveway in my bare feet*
3. *Be president of the homeowners' association*

It is amazing how you can go through half a century of life and never do something that apparently is not only a heck of lot of fun, but darn effective as well. Jeff tried to explain to me why it's important to aerate your lawn, but most of the explanation required that I actually listen. He did say something about golf greens that got my attention. And I kept hearing the word "plugs" which made me mildly interested because I once had a hair transplant. During the operation, the surgeon put over a thousand plugs in my head. My hair does look a lot thicker now, so I'm trying to keep an open mind about aeration.

Then I watched Norm try to aerate. Norm, who can only claim 5'8" in his wife's high heels, was being whipped into unspeakable contortions and had to pull the emergency button after he aerated Mark's newly paved driveway. Norm also chose to wear shorts, socks and sandals during this demonstration so we all got a pretty good picture of what would happen if people from a third world country went to Jack's Tool Rental on a Sunday morning.

After observing my neighbors gleefully involved in raising their testosterone levels, I agreed to try aeration myself. I declined doing my own lawn, having arranged several years ago for nine moles to do the job for me. I took hold of the handles, pressed the bar and was quickly propelled into action.

I guess I had never realized how exciting it would be to poke holes in a neighbor's lawn. It was the most fun I've ever had in my entire life. But four seconds was way long enough. I soon passed the privilege back to Jeff who happily aerated his yard again which, in my humble opinion, would be like mowing your lawn twice in a row.

Jeff is a heck of a guy, but I hope he returns that machine on Monday morning. Aerators make me nervous. They are huge, powerful and potentially dangerous. Someone could get hurt. Jeff could see I was uncomfortable with an aerator in the neighborhood, but he put my mind at ease. "Aerators don't poke holes in lawns. People poke holes in lawns," he told me.

That night, I slept like a baby.

Trouble Brewing

I recently assisted Gleaners Food Bank with some fund-raising efforts and they thanked me by asking a local beverage distributor (that's a liquor store) to donate a few exotic beers to me. Gleaners does an incredible job of feeding the hungry in central Indiana, but in my case they were thinking more of the thirsty.

Last night I opened up the last bottle in their gift box and was pleasantly surprised. The beer I sampled was light, crisp, full-bodied and nutty. I have no idea what some of those terms mean, but this is what you are supposed to say about beer.

But here's the kicker: The name of this delicious brew was "Three Stooges Beer." Now, I know a certain percentage of you are saying, "Do you think I was born yesterday? There's no such thing as Three Stooges Beer." The rest of you are saying, "Been drinking it for 25 years. But have you tried Curly Light?"

By the way, I have tried Curly Light. That was in the gift box, too.

The idea of drinking a beer with the Three Stooges on the bottle would have made four years of my liberal arts education that much more bearable. Why would any self-respecting college freshman curl up in his frat house with a Budweiser when he could get wasted with the world's funniest three-some?

One observation, please: Stranded in the Sahara Desert, mouth parched, near death—no woman would drink a Three Stooges Beer. You knew this, of course. We all instinctively know that women hate anything that has to do with the Three Stooges.

In fact, that's why most of you men have never heard of Three Stooges Beer. For years, a dedicated band of women have been buying this product and dumping it at chemical waste sites. You don't have to be a cultural anthropologist to know that once husbands get ahold of Three Stooges Beer, the nuclear family will be gone as we know it.

Personally, I think more products should be named after people. But I just don't like these made-up brand names likes Aunt Millie and Mrs. Paul. These are not real people; they are Madison Avenue creations. That just doesn't work for me.

I want real people. Einstein Bagels, for example. Now that's a name I can sink my teeth into. When I eat a bagel, at least I can see Albert Einstein in my mind's eye, shuffling downstairs in his robe for a bagel and cream cheese. I even have a slogan:

Einstein Bagels: Not just a recipe, a formula.
I'll tell you what I'd like to see—more food named after comedians. But once again, I don't think Madison Avenue would take the chance of alienating the woman shopper. I asked my wife if she'd ever buy Abbott and Costello Mayonnaise…
"Would there be Hellmann's on the shelf?"
"No Hellmann's."
"How about Kraft?"
"No, assume this is the only brand available."
"Well, in that case, I still wouldn't buy it. But I would buy Brad Pitt Olives. Do they make Mel Gibson Mustard?"
I'd also buy Laurel and Hardy Fishsticks. There's room in my fridge for Milton Berle Cream Cheese and a place in my pantry for Rodney Dangerfield Tomato Soup. Bob and Ray Tuna would make a dandy sandwich. I don't know about you, but wouldn't a container of Marx Brothers Yogurt really hit the spot right now?
Since I began writing this column, I have discovered that they have stopped producing Three Stooges Beer. No more Curly Light or Moe Extra Dry. Plans for Larry Draft have been scrapped. I am a lucky man. I have my health and a beautiful family. But I am unhappy to the point that I think I need to be carefully watched the next few days. My wife can't do it. She's out celebrating.

Fine for Parking

I have a bone to pick with the people who construct and set up parking lots. I never park in a handicapped space, though sometimes, I must admit, it seems there are just too many of them. I think there should be a more effective way of determining the number of spaces. At a skating rink the other day, all 14 handicapped spaces were unused. A friend told me there is actually a wheelchair hockey team. That's good enough for me.

The newest trend is reserved spaces for "Women who are pregnant" and "Women with small children." Again, I have no argument with this concept, but I do think there should be some new categories. As it is now, handicapped folks and women with kids seem to be getting most of the parking perks. I think men should have a few themselves. Here are the ones I would advocate at some of these huge mega-stores that sell everything:

Reserved Parking for Men Who Just Need Beer
It is amazing to me that no one has made men on a beer run a protected class. These guys have no malice, no vindictiveness, no grudge. They just want beer. They should have their own checkout lane that says: 44 BEERS OR LESS. Asking a guy with a six-pack of Miller Lite to stand in line behind a woman with a potted plant, a casserole dish, and panty hose seems cruel and unusual. At the very least, state law should allow these people to down a cold one while waiting in line.

Reserved Parking for Men Who Forgot the One Thing They Came For
This would be a boon to the guy who ran out to get a screwdriver and came home with a Weber Grill and 200 pounds of mulch. But no screwdriver. Coming back that second time is a source of great embarrassment and a nearby parking space can do wonders to reduce the humiliation. I would also fire anyone in a red jacket and a carnation who says, "You, again?"

Reserved Parking for Fathers Who Come Back for Their Children
I think there should be nearby parking for a dad who left his three kids in the toy section while he picked up a monkey wrench. Research shows that many of these fathers go home without the kids only to realize the children are missing when there are empty seats at dinner. These dads need a special

place to park so they can have quick access to all blood relatives in the store.

Reserved Parking for Men Seeking Feminine Products

Any man who will shop for personal items for his wife deserves a special place to park. My problem is I wouldn't know what to put on the sign. A lot of men asked by their wives to make this run have parked in handicapped spaces, leaned on the horn, jumped out of the car and done jumping jacks. All this with the hope that they would be arrested before they got inside the store.

Reserved Parking for Crooks

You hear all these stories about robbers who leave their credit cards or write a note to the bank teller on one of their own deposit slips. You know that some day, some idiot bent on robbing a store will see this sign and actually park in this space. Politicians and lawyers can also use this space.

Reserved Parking for Men Wearing Shorts, Long Black Socks and Loafers

I do feel sorry for these men. But why should we all suffer? Get them in the store and out of the store as fast as possible. I would also put on the parking sign: Sneakers and white socks FREE with every purchase. *(It won't work. Men like this can't take a hint.)*

Reserved Parking for Television Personalities with Beagles

I know this seems a bit self-serving, but here's how I differ from pregnant women: If you pull into the parking lot and I'm not using the space, it's all yours.

Thought for Food

My wife is getting very health conscious. I knew this would happen as soon as she got her AARP card. And to make matters worse she has subscribed to this publication called *Prevention Magazine*. It's about the same size as *Reader's Digest*, but it is absolutely nothing like *Reader's Digest*—with one exception: The word "digest" is all over the place.

You see, the purpose of this annoying little magazine is to basically give you the latest inane research on all the foods you can and can't eat. And my wife, who is too busy during the day to read all her periodicals, has decided to quote the magazine in the car on our way out to dinner.

"Wow, listen to this. Males who ate one handful of peanuts a day were 14% less likely to have a stroke."

"That may be true. I've never seen an elephant with a walker."

"Oh, here's one. They did a study with women

who wear completely natural fibers like 100% wool and cashmere. And guess what those women are 23% less likely to have?"

"A bad shopping spree?"

"No, osteoporosis. And listen to this. Men 50 and over—that's you—who eat fish just once a month are 30% less likely to have a heart attack and will live 10 years longer."

"Wow, now that *is* amazing!"

"Yes, and if fish didn't stink up the house, we could try that."

"Look, this is crazy. Where should we go for dinner?"

"Maybe Baskin Robbins. Listen to this: Chocolate is actually good for you. It says here that chocolate contains anti-oxidants and that it can prolong your life. But it also says that chocolate contains calories and fat that can cause obesity and heart disease. I guess that's not all good news.

"No, Dear. That's why they call it bitter-sweet chocolate."

"First of all, it's semi-sweet chocolate—and secondly, how come you get all the clever lines?"

"Keep reading."

"Okay. They did a study with 500 nurses. Half ate regular mayonnaise and half ate low-fat mayonnaise and guess what they found?"

"The low-fat mayonnaise nurses were more likely to marry a doctor?"

"No, wise guy, the regular mayonnaise nurses actually had lower cholesterol."

"Really?"

"And Dick, guess what the real mayonnaise nurses also had?"

"Not a clue."

"Better BLTs."

"That's not in the magazine."

"No, but now we're even on that chocolate come-back."

"Tell me more."

"Okay, according to this magazine, couples who eat out more than twice a week have a 12% greater chance of having a car accident."

"Put the magazine away, Mary Ellen."

"Let me ask you this, Dick. Do you get your pulse rate up to 180 at least once a day?"

"Yes. Three cups of coffee usually does the trick in the morning. Listening to you read this magazine has also been incredibly effective."

The other day I opened the mail and noticed that my wife had bought a copy of *The Prevention Cookbook*, which doesn't have quite the same allure to me as *The Joy of Cooking*. In this book, they not only tell you the number of calories and the amount of fat that each dish has, but they tell you how long you'll live if you eat that recipe every day for the rest of your life.

Here's their meatloaf recipe:

Half pound of no-fat sausage
Three oz. of soy milk
6 oz. of hummus
12 peanuts

2 oz. skim milk
1 cup wheat germ
3 leaves fresh chopped spinach

Mary Ellen made me mix this stuff up and form a hamburger patty; then she made me grill it outside on my Weber.

Was it good? I don't really know for sure. But the dog is going to live to be 100.

What's the Beef?

Well, I've got some bad news for Thomas Jefferson and Martin Luther King. They used to be tied at the top of my list of people I most admire, but then I read in the paper the other day about this guy who has eaten at least two Big Macs every day for 30 years. Donald Gorsky lives in Milwaukee, which is amazing. No, not the Milwaukee part, the living part. Let's go through this again: two Macs a day for 30 years, which, according to a group of high school students who have researched this, is the equivalent to 800 heads of lettuce, 523 pounds of cheese, 100 gallons of special sauce, 14 heads of cattle and several million sesame seeds. And he says he never gets sick. Except to his stomach.

You just have to give a guy like this some credit. Every health and diet book in the country would have predicted that this guy should have been in his McCoffin by now, but instead, the paper says he is healthy, robust and has actually fathered genetically viable children. And he broke a few other records, as well:

1. Most consecutive decades (4) for one individual to surpass the RDA for saturated fat for all of Wisconsin.

2. Person with most articles of clothing (26) with special sauce stains.

3. Longest living (living is the key word here, again) person to totally eliminate nine essential vitamins from his diet for 30 years without having traumatic cardio-vascular problems or a giant zit somewhere on his body.

4. Rumor has it he also ate 25 White Castles a day for 30 years, but he never mentions it because it's a disgusting habit and he's trying to quit. But here's my question: Did he actually start out trying to break this record, or, after 30 years of this unhealthy obsession, did he realize he might have eaten himself into the record books? I don't want to take anything away from the guy, but it's easy to throw darts and then draw the bull's eye.

I'm sure all of us have probably broken records, but we're not smart enough to figure out beforehand that some of our habitual behaviors actually belong in the record books. I made a list of some of the records I have probably set, but I fear there is no category for my accomplishments.

1. Every morning for 25 years, I have gotten in the shower, washed my face, stepped out of the shower to shave, then stepped back in the shower to rinse off my face. I have never wavered from this. Not

once. (No word from Guinness yet.)

2. For 40 years, every morning, I have put on a sock, then a shoe, then a sock, then a shoe. The only exception was April 14, 1978, when I spent too much time with a pitcher of margaritas (instead of doing my taxes) and ended up trying to put on a shoe first, then a sock (on the same foot), then another shoe and another sock. I e-mailed *Ripley's Believe It or Not*. I should hear any day.

3. And here's the big one. Every day since the election of Jimmy Carter, I have told a different knock-knock joke to someone. In total, I have told 14,600 knock-knock jokes. No repeats, no days off. No word back yet from *The Enquirer* on this one. They must be on a holiday break. Oh, one final note about Mr. Gorsky. He's a prison guard in Milwaukee. Apparently, when the inmates started chanting "NOT SALISBURY STEAK AGAIN," he wasn't very sympathetic.

The Free Press

If you paid for this book, I apologize. I say that because anyone with any persuasive powers can get a book for free. I don't mind telling this now, because for you, it's too late. Truth is, everyone wants a free book. I know from my last book, *Life in a Nutshell*.

Oh, nobody actually just came right out and said it. Instead, friends came up to me in the street and said: "Hey, Dick, I just heard about your book. I think that's great. You are so funny, so creative, so intelligent. How about a free copy?"

Come to think of it, they did just come right out and say it.

My writer friends have given me some tips for responses to, "Hey Dick, how about a free copy?"

"Hey Ralph, how about 13.95... plus tax?"

"Are you familiar with the concept of making a living?"

"Does the word 'invoice' ring a bell?"

"Sorry, I'm out of free copies. I just gave my last one to another person that I barely know."

"Isn't that funny? For a brief moment there I thought you were asking that after I worked every day for two years on this book, you wanted me to give you a free copy which would mean I'd have to reimburse the publisher which means it would cost me 14 bucks. Of course, I must have misunderstood you. What did you really say?"

I think people assume that the publisher gives me six or eight thousand copies to give away. The truth is I got 20 free copies. My mother got 18 at 14 bucks apiece, so I guess I do have a little flexibility with my really close friends.

The problem is that I have a rather strong personality, so people either think I'm a pretty neat guy—or they would prefer to live in a different time zone. Very few have mixed feelings. So there you have it. My friends think they deserve a free book. The others would rather buy a Firestone tire. I think you see the problem.

The funny thing about this is that there are certain businesses where FREE is sort of a given. When I go to Tim's Bar, I do expect a free beer every once in a while. But I seldom go into my local clothing store and expect Tony to say, "Hey Dick, good to see you. Sit down, have a sport coat." I know the guy at the post office as well as my own brother, but the words, "Dick, have a 34-cent stamp on me," are seldom heard. The lady at the jewelry store asked me for a free book, but when I asked her for a complimentary watch band, she seemed a bit put off.

The whole concept of free is kind of intriguing.

Take a look at some of these phrases...

FREE INSPECTION: What they do before they take advantage of you.

FREE LOVE: Not cheap, believe me.

50% FAT-FREE: Same amount of fat, but you have to eat twice as much.

FREE GIFT: Unlikely, and what's worse, redundant.

FREE TV: What you have won as long as you pay $300 in shipping and handling.

FREE LUNCH: Once unheard of, now available with a coupon as long as you buy the first overpriced lunch.

FREE CHECKING: A fancy name for giving you 2% interest a year instead of 5%.

FREE INSTALLATION: Generally means they'll get you on the monthly fee.

FREE-STANDING CONDOMINIUM: $300,000

FREE ADVICE: Worth every penny.

FREE SPEECH: If you just count the Optimist Clubs, Lions Clubs and Elks Lodges, I've given about 600 of these.

If this all seems a bit disjointed, I apologize. You see, I wrote it with a slightly different method. I simply sat down in a big comfy chair and let my mind wander. This is called free association. And now you've paid the price.

Whipping Boy

My wife is trying to kick it up a notch. Before you misunderstand this phrase, let me explain that this is an expression used by Chef Emeril Lagasse who does cooking demonstrations on *Good Morning America*. He uses this expression "kicking it up a notch" whenever he adds a spice to a dish that could potentially dissolve the septum in your nose.

My wife is a big fan of Emeril's, which is kind of odd because she is not a big fan of cooking. Let's face it, if you like to watch fishing shows, you probably love fishing. If you like to watch bowling on TV, you are probably a bowler. If you watch bullfighting, then… okay, no theory is perfect. Even Einstein's Theory of Relativity had a few black holes in it.

But let's get back to Emeril. His flamboyant style actually motivates my wife to try new and exciting things in the kitchen. His cooking is magic, and my wife is one of the viewers who have been tricked.

Here's how the ruse works: Emeril decides to prepare a dish that has somewhere in the neighborhood of 28 ingredients. Unfortunately, none of these ingredients is in YOUR neighborhood. Of course, Emeril has a staff of 26 ABC interns and three grad students from the Wharton School of Business who do nothing but travel the country shopping for these exotic herbs and vegetables.

Once Emeril has these ingredients, they need to be chopped, sliced, diced, cubed and shaved. For this, Emeril has another throng of people to help him—including Diane Sawyer—who is secretly so desperate to host *Monday Night Football* that she'll do anything to impress her bosses.

Now comes the show. On the table, Emeril displays the exotic herbs, spices and mushrooms that took his staff four months to acquire. Everything on the table is now in tiny bowls, measured to a microgram—the work of two more seniors from MIT.

In walks Emeril, cool as a cucumber. But not just any cucumbera cucumber from the foothills of Peru that only grows between coffee plants, giving it a piquant aroma... See what I mean?

Emeril, who's got about two minutes to make this exquisite dish, spends the first minute whipping his audience into a gastronomic frenzy. The crowd, drooling in anticipation, has been pureed into such a state that you have to wonder if this is their first meal or their last.

Now Emeril goes to work. If you can call it work. "So you take this and throw it in the pan with this, then you add this plus a little of this, stir in some of this, a pinch of that, a bowl of this, a cup of this... and BAM! There you have it... Veal Remoulade a la

Astoria, an exquisite dish you can make in two minutes."

Millions of men and women watching this break out in applause. How can this be? How can you make Veal Remoulade a la Astoria in only two minutes? It can't be. But it must be. It was on television.

By evening, men and women across the nation are convinced that they too can create this very same masterpiece in the kitchen in a matter of moments... possibly during a commercial break. Busy husbands and wives rush home from their jobs and download the recipe from the *Good Morning America* Website. Then they stare at the recipe and realize that no mortal could possibly prepare this in one evening. My wife felt defeated...

"Dick, would you be real disappointed if we just had hamburgers?"

"Burgers are fine. In fact, let's kick it up a notch. Let's make it cheeseburgers."

Being in a Vegetable Stew

I'm no health nut. But I try to live my life somewhere vaguely within the nutritional guidelines
established by what I envision as a panel of chubby
Harvard nutrition experts still grumpy over not getting into medical school.

So while I find compliance with some of the
guidelines an annoyance, I do welcome the assis-
tance to living my life based on scientific facts. Now
that I've gotten that bunch of baloney out of the
way, let's be honest here.

I can exercise five times a week. I can cut down on
fat. I can eat three fruits a day. I can even choke
down eight glasses of water (if you count scotch
and water and teeth brushing). I'll even eat cod
once a week for all you big omega fat fans. But I
can't do 11 vegetables a day. No way. No how.

Oh, you haven't heard this? The new nutritional
food pyramid, a structure that would make
Pharaohs roll over in their tombs, now suggests that

the average person needs between nine and eleven portions of fresh vegetables every day. I can't do this. I have a job. I have a family. Oh yeah, and I hate vegetables.

Let's talk about this. If there are no children present, permit me to make this point: When God invented sex he made the act pleasurable; if he hadn't, people would have skipped it and gone fishing instead. And where would we all be now?

So what happened with broccoli? I mean, if God can make a waterfall and a hurricane, why can't broccoli taste like mint chip ice cream? I don't want to be critical, but when you've got the gift of miracles, flaunt it! It's just that if all these things are supposed to be so good for you, why weren't they made better tasting? If vegetables all tasted like french fries, I'd be 10 pounds thinner. And wouldn't you just love to hear your kid say at a fast food place: May I have a cheeseburger and a large order of beets? Music to my ears.

But back to my dilemma. Could I eat 11 servings of vegetables in one day?

My wife suggested that instead of seeing vegetables as tiny pieces of tasteless greenery, I should find some creative way of eating them, to make them more palatable. It sparked a brilliant idea. So brilliant, in fact, that I would like to share with you my plan for getting in your 11 veggies a day. I'm going to call it the State Fair Diet. I was there last summer and saw very few people at the salad concession, so I'm dedicating the diet to them.

Breakfast
Two Bloody Marys (with V-8 Juice and celery
sticks)
One piece of plain carrot cake
One Kosher pickle
Total Veggies: 4

Lunch
One Bloomin' Onion (Outback Steakhouse)
Two pieces of zucchini bread with vegetable
cream cheese
One cup of salsa
Total veggies: 4

Dinner
Two Easter Eggs (colored with vegetable dye)
Three pieces of cream cheese carrot cake
Deep-fried corn fritters with ketchup
One martini with two olives
Total veggies: 8

Wow! That's 16 servings. But just to be safe, I
think I'll have another martini. You can't be too
healthy.

Filtering Information

I was changing the light bulb above the stove the other day and smacked my head on the bottom of the microwave. I had never been under the microwave before, so I was shocked to find the following inscription affixed to the bottom of the appliance: Please clean the microwave filters at least once a month.

Who even knew that a microwave had filters? I don't know what those filters do, but apparently they require some pretty serious maintenance. I got out the service manual and it said that frequent cleaning would enhance the performance of the microwave. For 15 years I have been putting a Stouffer's Frozen Lasagna in this microwave every Friday night and hitting HIGH. And 780 times in a row, it's come out piping hot six minutes later. This is a streak even Joe DiMaggio would have envied. I don't mess with success. Joltin' Joe, change his stance in the middle of the season? I think not.

I did a little checking since this incident and I have discovered that I also have filters in my furnace. Two of them, in fact. I also have a filter in the clothes dryer and one on my lawn mower. I have one on the vacuum cleaner. Apparently there's one in my air conditioner. Next thing you now, I'll find out there's one in my car. I suspect all these filters are clamoring for a monthly change. I've neglected them. But I'm a busy guy. If you're a filter, don't expect my undivided attention.

Finding the time to do monthly maintenance on all your household appliances requires a very special kind of person. A person with no friends, family, sex life or means of transportation would probably be a good candidate. And how do you remember this stuff? Teeth cleanings and medical checkups are hard enough. I've had a Post-it Note on my fridge for five years that says: TETANUS SHOT, JUNE 2007.

The other day, just for fun, I got out all the manuals I could find from the various gadgets and appliances that we have around the house to see just how far behind the Wolfsies are in preventive maintenance. I was a little nervous about this whole process because it was beginning to look like an Andy Rooney commentary.

VCR: "Heads should be cleaned monthly," it says. I have never cleaned a VCR head in my life. In college I cleaned my own head only once a month. It says you need to buy a head cleaner. I hate to do that with my birthday right around the corner.

DESK RADIO: The directions say: If radio's dirty, wipe with a mild soapy solution. (I say if your radio is dirty, change stations.)

SNOWBLOWER: Maintain each season by removing blades and sharpening. I'm against sharp blades on snowblowers. The last thing we need are snowblower murderers.

ELECTRIC TOOTHBRUSH: "Once a month, take a Q-tip and clean the tiny plugs at the bottom of the appliance." They must be kidding. If I had the patience and dexterity to take a Q-tip and clean tiny plugs, I could brush my teeth the old-fashioned way.

FISHING REEL: According to the directions on my fishing reel, you are supposed to "take apart the reel periodically and lubricate the parts." What kind of person would have the patience to sit in a chair and just oil tiny little parts? Oh yeah...a fisherman.

MY EXERCISE BIKE: No joke, here's what it says: "Check tension monthly or fly wheel band will loosen and your workout will be less strenuous." Wow, there's a motivating reason to do preventive maintenance.

ELECTRIC PENCIL SHARPENER: The blades on this device will dull after approximately 20,000 uses. Blades cannot be sharpened. Please discard the unit and replace.

My kind of maintenance!

Palm Monday

I'm one of those people who make a list every day on a mini legal pad. Nowadays, this is kind of old school. Even kids are walking around with these things called Palm Pilots. This gives a person a false sense of organization. I had one for a few weeks and I was disappointed to discover that even with a $300 contraption in my palm, I still ended up with appointments in Greenwood and Carmel at exactly the same time. What a rip-off!

I have never been a big fan of the gimmicky stuff. I remember kicking and screaming back in the '70s about this one new-fangled invention. I refused to be suckered into something that was clearly just a high-tech fad. My girlfriend was a bit put off...

"Dick, I think you're being a little stubborn. This is a great convenience and a time saver. I know you're not technically gifted, but I think Post-it Notes may catch on."

Lately, however, I must admit that the palm pilot has begun to intrigue me. That's because I am find-ing that more and more often I write something on my legal pad and then I have no idea what it says or what it means. This comes from the fact that my handwriting is pretty rotten to begin with, my eyesight is getting worse—and so is my memory. Here's a recent example that stumped me. It was at the top of my legal pad with a star next to it.

*PRESENT/ SHIRLEY/ KIDS

I didn't have a clue what it meant. I don't even know a Shirley. At least, I don't think so.

"Mary Ellen, do we know a Shirley?"

"Shirley who?"

"Well, this is helpful. I don't know Shirley who. That's the problem."

I tried having a conversation with this mythical person, hoping it would ring a bell. I didn't know my wife was listening.

"Well, if it isn't Shirley... Shirley... Shirley. Well, good to see you again Shirley... Shirley... Shirley. So, Shirley... Shirley... Shirley, how's the family?

"Dick, I don't know who you are talking to, but that's a rotten Cary Grant impersonation. Try saying Judy, instead."

It was starting to drive me crazy. It was obviously Shirley's kids' birthdays and I sure would hate to forget an important occasion like that. I wouldn't want to ruin our relationship. Whoever she is.

I decided to call Channel 8. There are a couple hundred people there. One must be a Shirley.

"Channel 8. May I help you?"

"Hi, Marge. It's Dick Wolfsie. Is Shirley there?"

"Shirley who? We have three Shirleys."

It's obvious that when you have a problem like this, no one wants to cooperate. I didn't know who Shirley was. I didn't know why she and her kids were on my list. I did know one thing: Her children were not getting a present. At least not from me. Not this year.

Then yesterday, this appeared on my list:

BOWL/ MILK/ JOHN

Another stumper. Was I supposed to pick up milk after I went bowling? Did my neighbor, John, want to borrow a bowl of milk? I didn't have a clue. Fortunately, some of these things do have a way of working out. Later that night, my wife walked in from work...

"Hi, Dick. I hope you remembered to put a bowl of milk in the bathroom for the cats."

BINGO!

And finally, this was on my list:

SEND PACKAGE (VERY IMP'T)

I didn't have a package. I searched the entire house. No package. How can you send a package (imp't) when you don't have a package? I was desperate.

"Mary Ellen, did you return that package for me?"

"What package?"

"Oh, you know, that very important package that was lying around the house just waiting to be sent."

"I don't know what you're talking about, but you

better get dressed or you'll be late."

"Where am I going?"

"To Shirley, Indiana. Aren't you going to present an award to some kids up there? Didn't you write it down?"

"Yes, of course, of course. But how did you remember?"

"I used a Post-it Note."

Grrrrilled Cheese

I don't know who invented the grilled cheese sandwich, but I'm sure that if he's been listening to the TV and radio lately, he's turning over in his grave. Turning over is an important aspect of a grilled cheese sandwich, so if he is turning over, I'm sure he's timing it exactly right.

Why would I write an entire piece about grilled cheese sandwiches? Because a new ad campaign is threatening this distinctly American delight, and I'm not happy about it.

The ads proclaim a contest for the "Best Grilled Cheese Sandwich." Finalists will be asked to prepare their favorite version. But hidden in this seemingly innocent promotion is a fundamental flaw. You see, the beauty of a grilled cheese sandwich is that its ingredients belie the fact that you can't improve upon the basic recipe. The ingredients for a grilled cheese sandwich are simple:

American cheese
White bread
Butter

I'm warning you people who are considering entering this contest: Do not mess with this recipe. I've seen Judge Judy put people in the slammer for less.

As soon as you try to make a better grilled cheese sandwich, it's not a grilled cheese sandwich anymore. Instead, it's a cheese sandwich that's grilled with artichokes. Or it's a cheese sandwich that's grilled with honey-maple bread. Or it's a cheese sandwich with onion and tomato. Or, it's a cheese sandwich that's grilled, made with low-fat cheddar cheese. *THESE ARE NOT GRILLED CHEESE SANDWICHES. THESE ARE NOT GRILLED CHEESE SANDWICHES. THESE ARE NOT GRILLED CHEESE SANDWICHES.*

As you can see, I'm starting to heat up about this.

I think a lot of this comes from childhood. My mother made a great BLT sandwich. Her tuna sandwiches really hit the spot. With these dishes, there was very little room for innovation. As a child, you don't want surprises. When's the last time you saw TODAY'S SPECIAL on a kids' menu?

Don't misunderstand. Just because the recipe is simple, doesn't mean that the preparation is easy. The pan needs to be heated to just the right temperature, the butter needs to quietly nestle in the center of the pan, then trickle to the edges before it browns. The pan must then be covered as each side of the bread browns and the cheese melts perfectly. HEY, ARE YOU WRITING THIS DOWN?

By the way, I used to feel the same way about lemonade. You can call it raspberry lemonade, but it's not lemonade. You can call it peach lemonade, but it's not lemonade. Yeah, that used to drive me crazy. But I got over it. You can only fight so many battles.

You know, I'm not done griping about this grilled cheese thing. Who's going to enter this contest, anyway? Probably a bunch of Generation Xers who think that if you slather salsa over something it becomes a health food. Or maybe a panel of "30-Somethings" who think that a wheel of Brie on toasted sourdough bread in some way can be loosely interpreted as a grilled cheese sandwich. GRRRRRRR...

Look, let me try this again: American cheese, white bread, butter. Here's my e-mail address: Wolfsie@aol.com. What part of that recipe is confusing you?

I nurtured a grilled cheese sandwich for my 14-year-old son the other day. It was a thing of beauty. I marveled at it in the pan. It was as close to the Platonic ideal as possible: uniformly browned, cheese melted to perfection, an aroma that had put the dog into some kind of hypnotic trance.

"How's that grilled cheese sandwich, Brett?"

"Oh, pretty good, Dad. Could you pass the ketchup?"

"I could, if you want to go to your room for the

rest of your life."

I realize I'm taking this whole thing a bit too seriously. And I think I eat grilled cheese sandwiches way too often. In fact, I went for a medical checkup the other day and I got some bad news...

"Dick, I've looked at your test results and this grilled cheese obsession is creating a problem with your blood."

"Oh, dear. Is it raising my cholesterol?"

"No, your blood pressure."

Cheese Whiz

I'm just about to leave for a trip to Boston and I still have a newspaper column to write. I'm really short on time, so I checked my agreement with my editor and was reminded that my column has to contain a minimum of 600 words. My last column was close to 700—so I've been working way too hard. But this week I may have to take advantage of my contractual agreement because I'm really pressed for time.

Problem is that I needed a topic that only required 600 words. I skimmed through the papers this morning and as luck would have it, guess what I discovered?: It's National Goat Cheese Month.

How time flies. Seems like just yesterday I was celebrating National Goat Cheese Month with some of my closest friends. Has it really been a year?

I sometimes wonder how goat cheese got an entire month. I don't want to insult goat cheese lovers (or goats, for that matter), but I don't think goat cheese regalia deserves four weeks.

I figure with a good party planner and some forethought you can celebrate everything about goat cheese in a day. Maybe two hours. But I think the problem is that "National Goat Cheese Two Hours" just doesn't have the same ring to it.

You're wondering where this column is headed. You've just said to your wife, "Doris, where's he going with this goat cheese thing? You can't write 600 words about goat cheese." I'm hoping Doris will say, "You're selling the guy short, Herb. Sure he can do it. I've seen him write about even dumber things. Let's cut him a little slack."

Of course I can do it. And I'm not going to take the easy way out by talking about National Pickle Month, which has been a total disaster ever since the Republicans got the White House. Or National Peanut Butter Month, which started slowly but spread over the years. I won't even mention National Kite Month, which had trouble getting off the ground, but... well, I think you get the picture.

No, this is about National Goat Cheese Month. And I'm sticking to it. (I think that last line would have been better during National Peanut Butter Month.)

Okay, you ask, how did goat cheese get an entire month? Is there a goat cheese lobby? Maybe you don't need an act of Congress. Maybe you just say, "This is National Goat Cheese Month and if you don't like it, well, just get your own month."

I have a feeling that most of the months are taken. In fact, I have a sneaking suspicion that while we're all out whooping it up for goat cheese, the

American Dental Association is celebrating their month. It's probably also National Mandolin Month. And National Osteoporosis Month. How can you expect people to focus and have a really good time when there are so many distractions?

Now that I know it's National Goat Cheese Month, I don't want to fritter it away (I'd do that during National Apple Month.) I mean, how many Junes do I have left? My wife and I are planning to celebrate by going out for dinner. There's a place down the street called "Chuck E. Cheese's." It's very nice... if you're seven years old. Or if your serum cholesterol is below 100.

After that we'll... or maybe we'll go down to... how about a nice evening of... See what I mean? You can't fill a month.

Doris was right. I did write 600 words about goat cheese, which is the very minimum I'm allowed to turn in.

Six hundred. Exactly.

Sick Humor

I never get sick. In 10 years at Channel 8, I have never missed a day of work due to illness. So when I got hit with the flu this past week, I was totally out of practice.

I was always under the impression that when you had the flu or a very bad cold, this misery was compensated by the fact that someone would fawn over you for 10 days in a row, bring you hot soup, fluff up your pillow and say things like, "Are you sure you're okay?" and "Can I get you anything?"

This is what I used to think. Then I got married. It's not that my wife isn't a sympathetic, sensitive person. She cries during old movies when a small boy waves good-bye to his dad going off to war. She weeps when she watches the news and a mother tells her plight of raising ten adopted children. I have seen her sob when Peyton Manning is sacked. There's not a great deal of sympathy left for my draining sinuses.

As I said, I don't get sick very often, but when I do get sick, I really want to milk it for everything it's worth. Sighing, groaning and moaning are just a few techniques that I use to remind my family that I am upstairs in the guest bedroom and that I desperately need attention.

This past weekend I was in the middle of my routine: low guttural sounds and heavy sighing and breathing—punctuated by a very effective cough, if I do say so myself. Suddenly, I heard the front door slam. My wife had gone out to do some errands. When she got back four hours later, I was very upset...

"Mary Ellen, you left the house and never said good-bye. Suppose I needed water, or soup, or a paramedic?"

"I don't think you're that sick."

"Why do you say that?"

"Let's see. Since I've been gone you have apparently managed to make yourself lunch, go out for the mail, do your laundry and clean out the garage."

"I also repainted the guestroom. Look, I got bored. But now that you are home, I'm going to go back upstairs to groan and sniffle. If you're not too busy right now, could you pull up a chair at the bottom of the stairs and just listen for awhile?"

My final hope for real sympathy was my son, Brett. I walked past him and let out a deep moan, then a raspy cough.

"What's the matter, Dad? You don't sound so good."

"Let's see. Do you remember the other day when

you woke up for school and said you were all achy and had a headache and felt just plain lousy?"

"Yes, I remember."

"That's exactly what's happening with me."

"You mean you're faking?"

Getting sympathy from family is sometimes tough, but there are a few sure-fire methods with friends and colleagues...

"Hey Dick, it's Tim. Heard you were under the weather."

"Yeah, the doctor says it's influenza."

"INFLUENZA! Oh my God! I thought it was just the flu. Have you got all your papers in order?"

I must admit that my dog, Barney, is quite understanding. If I could just get my wife to cuddle up like a beagle, put her cute little nose right next to me and look at me with those sad, droopy eyes, I'd be the happiest guy in the world. I know a lot of you men have your own fantasies, but I'm sticking with that one.

I can't really blame my wife for all this lack of attention. She just never developed an effective personal strategy for dealing with illness. When miserable, she usually retreats to the bedroom with a cup of tea, a good book, and several boxes of Kleenex. Then she closes the door and suffers silently.

Some people just don't know how to be sick.

Calendar Boy

It was on the front seat of my car. I was on the way home and I made one stop. I never took it out of the car. When I ran into the dry cleaners, I'm sure some career criminal ransacked my car and stole... my appointment book.

There were other things in the car he (or she) could have stolen. There was my dog, Barney. But most crooks are either cat or ferret lovers. There was a $24.00 sirloin steak. Very few thugs are vegetarians, so I must have gotten lucky.

There were also 250 brand new black-and-white publicity photos of me. I'd have felt better if the scum had taken just one. I counted four times. They're all there.

But he did take my appointment calendar. What in heaven's name would a hood like that do with my day planner? I hope they catch the guy and the judge makes him do a few things on my calendar for the next year.

And if you (and you know who YOU are) are reading this, here's some advice as you live my life for the next 12 months. You're lucky these are the only ones I remember.

May 10: TAKE BARNEY TO VET

He'll know where he's going, too. He'll shake and shed his hair and probably get sick in your car—assuming it is your car.

June 14: 21st ANNIVERSARY

Last year was our 20th and it cost me six grand to go to Ireland. This year you could just get my wife a nice scarf. You got off cheap. I wish you had stolen the book last year.

July 6: WIFE'S 50th BIRTHDAY

She expects a surprise party. I hope you know how to throw a big bash. Don't forget. Forgetting number 50 would be, well, criminal.

July 8: BRETT'S 14th BIRTHDAY

I'm just warning you that he's at the in-between age. Boys go from an interest in Legos to an interest in legs about this time. Don't forget to invite Brett's friend Seth. You won't like Seth. But you deserve Seth.

August 4: COLONOSCOPY

I keep putting this off, but it is on my calendar. I don't think crooks like you care about their colons, but I have it scheduled. Dr. Payne is very gentle. Have fun!!

August 24: SCHOOL BEGINS

Brett, my 14-year-old, starts school. The first day of school is pretty rough on parents. You'll have to go to several PTO meetings. And plan to spend a couple hundred on books and school supplies. Abercrombie T-shirts are 40 bucks. You shouldn't have given up your second-story job.

October 25: FALL BREAK

Do you have kids? You know, little future ex-cons running around your house? You'll need to take my son to The Chicago Field Museum. Don't try to weasel out of this—even though you are a weasel. One warning: if you try to sneak in, my kid will tell on you.

November 2: SPEECH FOR NATIONAL ALLIANCE OF SECRETARIES

You might like this. Three hundred women, all of whom have had far too many cocktails and are looking for a few chuckles. I bet they'd love to hear some firsthand stories about robbing parked cars. You'll be a laugh riot.

December 15: CHRISTMAS GIFT DEADLINE

In the back of my calendar are all the people I send gifts and cards to. Please be generous. It's bad enough that you have stolen my calendar, you don't have to make me look like a tightwad.

February 10: VISIT MOM IN NEW YORK

I want to be clear on this. You are not to visit YOUR mother; you are to visit MY mother. My mother raised her kids to be honest. Never to steal. And to be punctual. Which is why I HAD an appointment book. And you are to spend the entire five days sitting at home talking to her. Or rather, her talking to you. And you are to clean your plate.

Well, ya big jerk, those are just the highlights I remember. Don't forget that you have to go to work every morning at 3:30 a.m. You'll be on TV in front of about 100,000 people.

I'll be watching!

Proverbial Nonsense

Recently, I used an expression in one of my newspaper columns that may have puzzled you. The expression was "second-story man."

My good friend, Heidi, who often proofreads my columns, e-mailed me to say that she had never heard the expression, and in case I cared, neither had any of the people she'd gone to college, high school or day camp with. Heidi is very thorough.

A second-story man is a burglar who enters windows from—here's the easy part—the second floor. If you want to know more, you could look it up. Or, if you live in a bad neighborhood, you could just look up. Or you could even watch an entire movie about a second-story man, *To Catch a Thief*, with Cary Grant. In that movie, Grant was the kind of second-story man that women unlocked their windows for, but that's another story... so to speak.

But back to words and expressions. At first, I was kind of shocked that so many people had never heard this term, but a little reflection changed my thinking. There is always the remote chance that each time the expression "second-story man" came up, Heidi was in the ladies' room, windsurfing, or proofreading a cereal box.

This could happen with many words or phrases. I remember I was almost 30 years old when I first heard the word "gams," a sexy term for legs. Close friends, especially male, were astonished that I had never heard the word gams. "You've led a very sheltered life," my friend Craig said to me. But I don't think that is the explanation at all. I just think that every time the word gams came up I was playing golf or vacuuming out my car. Or I may have been in a neighborhood bar looking at a nice set of gams. I just didn't know it at the time.

My theory is that all of us, by the basic laws of chance, have missed something very simple in life. Something that virtually everyone else is aware of. You just weren't around when the phrase came up. Examples of this are everywhere. Recently I took a survey of 100 people, people with college educations—men and women who paid good money to go to fine schools. Here's what I found: Out of 100 people, two never heard the expression, "It takes two to tango." One woman with a Ph.D. from Stanford was baffled by "The straw that broke the camel's back." I know that you're tempted to quit reading this because it is so weird, but there is a little part of you that knows I'm on to something.

Now, I don't mean to scare you, but you could be

walking around now completely unaware of a common phrase that everyone in the world knows about but you. Why? Look, I can't explain this whole thing again. Please read paragraphs five and six one more time.

Okay, I'm not through beating this dead horse. Now, some of you are saying, "Gee, that's an odd expression. I've never heard that before." See? That's exactly my point. Someday you'll go on *Who Wants To Be A Millionaire?* and Regis will ask you (for 100 lousy bucks) to finish the saying "Every cloud has a...." And you'll be the only dunce ever to need a lifeline for the first question. Why? Why? Paragraphs five and six, please.

Okay, I'm done. It's bad enough I'm driving this into the ground, but as the old expression goes, "It's better than shaving a rangostat."

Ethical Times

Because I am originally a New Yorker, I read the *New York Times* every Sunday morning. Okay, I don't actually read the whole thing. I pull out the sports section, the "News of the Week in Review" and the magazine section. This leaves about six pounds of newspaper, which is two pounds of ads, three pounds of classifieds, and one pound of depressing news about the Bronx.

Once I accept the fact that I can't answer a single clue in the Sunday crossword puzzle, I turn to my favorite column, "The Ethicist," by Randy Cohen. Randy takes questions from people on moral and ethical issues, then responds with his own view from a cell in Terre Haute, Indiana, where he is doing twenty-five-to-life.

I'm kidding, of course, but Randy does have a great job. I told some friends that if I ever run out of ideas for my weekly humor column, this is the gig I want. And trust me, I'll be a lot easier on you than Randy, who once told a reader that when you leave a restaurant and it's pouring outside, it's wrong to take the last umbrella from the coat room, even if the umbrella looks exactly like yours. Yeah, right!

Here's how I'd answer some common questions:

DEAR DICK,
I am a big Pacers fan, but I can't afford the tickets. So, I applied for a job cleaning the stands after the games. After my regular job, I go to the Fieldhouse, clock in, go down to the expensive seats, grab a beer and watch the game. After the game, I go right home. I have never done a lick of work, but I did make $14,000 last year. Is this ethical?
Frank

DEAR FRANK,
I like your ingenuity, but what you are doing is wrong. However, I am going to cut you some slack. After all, you're a loyal Pacers fan and you are holding down two jobs.

DEAR DICK,
My neighbor, Jeff, goes out every Saturday morning like clockwork and fills up his little red two-gallon container at the gas station so he can fuel up his lawn mower. But his mower only takes one gallon. Saturday night, I sneak into his garage and fill my mower with the remaining gas. I have been doing this for five years. He has never caught on. Is this stealing?
Joe

DEAR JOE,

I have searched the law books, talked to experts and even looked into my own heart and yes, this is stealing. Here's my advice: Rather than admit your past indiscretions—which could ruin your close relationship with Jeff—why not secretly mow his lawn every Saturday night at around 2 a.m.? This will allay your guilt. And based on your letter, I doubt he'll even notice.

DEAR DICK,

I have worked for a downtown steakhouse my entire life. I have never done anything dishonest, with one exception. Every night, just to see if I can get away with it, I put a bottle of ketchup in my purse when I go home. Now as I near my 25th anniversary retirement party, I have 6,000 bottles of ketchup in my pantry. Should I return them? I'm starting to feel guilty.

Rosie

DEAR ROSIE,

First of all, the people in your hometown should be grateful you don't work at the local Savings and Loan. Returning the ketchup all at once could arouse suspicion. I suggest you return the condiments in exactly the same methodical manner in which you borrowed them. There will be a 25-year delay in your retirement party. Sorry about that.

DEAR DICK,

I work at your TV station. Every Friday, someone brings in a delicious corned beef sandwich and puts it in the community fridge. I take the sandwich apart, eat half the corned beef, fluff the meat back up and put the sandwich back together. This loser has never caught on. What do you say?

Tony

DEAR TONY,
First of all, you sleaze bag, it's pastrami, not corned beef. And I am now in favor of televised executions.

(note: Send all ethical questions to Wolfsie@aol.com. Due to the volume of mail that Dick gets, all questions will be answered personally!)

Mail Ego

I don't like things going on in my house while I'm sleeping. Sometimes I hear my refrigerator doing its own maintenance at night. No one has ever fully explained to me what those noises are, but I believe that life in your kitchen should end at bedtime. My gas water heater is having some kind of seance in the basement, and my VCR is doing a self-appraisal which continues even if I rip the plug out of the wall. I'm even suspicious of my vacuum cleaner, but at three in the morning I'm just too scared to open the closet.

I also have my suspicions about my son's Nintendo game. But I don't make false accusations against something with that much fire power.

I used to belong to a labor union, so I am very sensitive to anything that smacks of overtime. I'm pretty hard on my appliances and when they put in a good 12-14 hours, they're off the hook for the rest of the evening. When I hear noise in my house after midnight, it better be the cats or a burglar. I don't want my dishwasher on time-and-a-half.

Sometimes at night I hear my computer grinding away. I know it's up to something and the result is that I've lost a great deal of trust in its operation. I am convinced that at night it has a hidden life. At first I thought there was something going on between my computer and the water heater, but now I'm pretty sure that my printer is in on this. My printer already had me suspicious because it always has a hissy-fit before it actually prints.

But back to the computer. Because I've lost confidence in it, I test my e-mail every day by sending myself a message entitled TEST. The other morning, instead of TEST, I simply typed my name: DICK WOLFSIE. Then I sent it to myself. At least I thought I did. But by mistake, I also sent it to 150 people on my newspaper column e-mail list. When these folks opened the e-mail, all it said was DICK WOLFSIE.

The initial result of this gaffe was that I heard from people I had not heard from in two years. There are other people who read my hysterical, brilliantly conceived column every week who have never had the decency to write or call before. Here's what some folks had to say:

(The e-mail addresses have been changed to protect the not-so-funny)

BARMAN (my nephew): Hey, Uncle Dick. Funny stuff. The best you've written.

YO926: Thanks for sending me your name. I used it all day today. I'm sending it back. Mine works better.

TOOCUTE: I don't get it. And I've read it three times.

M78STUD: Hey, Dick. Thanks for sending me your name. I've sent it to 500 lawyers with a note that some rich guy rear-ended you in his Lexus.

HUB67BUB: Thanks for sending me your name. But I accidentally deleted it. Please send me another one.

BRUCE: Not one of your best columns, Dick. No plot and only one weak character.

Lo987: Hi, Dick. Thanks for sending me your name. I'm sending you mine, also: LOIS! Aren't computers just the best?

SEAFOX (my brother): It's always about you, isn't it?

M670JAY: Well written. Thank goodness for spell-check.

UPSI: Please take me off your e-mail list. I have a 10-year-old.

H76TIG: You need some light outpatient therapy.

MAMAW (my mom): That's nice. Does that count as a phone call?

I'm not really sure how to end this column. Let's just say that if I should ever send you my name again via e-mail, please treat it with some reverence. It's over 50 years old and has traveled around the country several times. It deserves a little respect. And feel free to send me your name. I look forward to reading it.

School Daze

This school year began with the usual flurry of activity. My wife, Mary Ellen, went out to all the stores looking for cool, with-it clothes for Brett. She stood in long lines and tried to shop all the sales. Then she got the school supplies list and spent all day looking for all the right pens, notebooks, and calculators. Then she spent an entire day getting Brett registered and meeting with his teachers. Then she took him for a haircut. It was rough. The poor kid was just tuckered out.

It's tough on kids today. My son took three art courses over the summer, traveled to Ireland, went whitewater rafting and played tennis in the cool of the evening. He played high-tech video games in our air conditioned basement and swam in the neighborhood pool. I think if you want kids to be excited about school starting, you have to make sure they have a rotten summer. I didn't do a very good job of that. I'll do better next year.

When I was a kid, I actually looked forward to school starting. It's not that I was such a wonderful student, but after spending the summer playing little league baseball in a wool uniform and batting 134, I was ready for school.

Thinking about school has brought back a few vivid memories...

I took French when I was in high school. My first-year French teacher always bragged he could speak 32 languages. I don't think that was enough because no one in the class ever knew what he was talking about. My second year French teacher said she spoke 12 languages. Once we caught my first year French teacher and second year French teacher together in a car after school. With 44 languages at their disposal, neither of them seemed to be talking.

There was also this course called P.A.D. This was an abbreviation for Problems in American Democracy. It was taught by the worst teacher at New Rochelle High School. None of the kids went to the class. I guess that was the problem they were talking about.

My history teacher at New Rochelle was Mrs. Weinstein. She had taught my father 25 years earlier when he went to the same school. This puts a lot of pressure on a kid. My father was very, very smart. He was the class valedictorian and then went on to Cornell. I think Mrs. Weinstein confused my father and me. I know she confused me. I never knew what she was yelling about. I also think Mrs. Weinstein was a little behind in grading papers. I got two of my father's papers back.

Four years later, I went back to my high school to

teach and now Mrs. Weinstein was my supervisor. I think there should be a law against stuff like this happening. I can't explain why. But I know I'm right.

My favorite class in high school was English. My teacher, Mr. Mahoney, taught me the pleasures of parsing. In three years of high school, I never mastered how to do a geometric proof or the skill to balance a chemical equation. But if you gave me a sentence with a compound subject, a gerund and an indirect object, in less than 10 seconds I could suck all the charm out of that prose by diagramming it to death.

While some men have memories of a misspent youth, mine are of misplaced modifiers. I have no memory of mixed feelings about my childhood, only mixed metaphors. In fact, if I have any regrets at all, it's that we don't live in New Rochelle, New York, any more. I think my son and Mrs. Weinstein would really hit it off.

Closet Case

I read somewhere in one of those gossipy magazines that Bill Gates' wife, Melinda, thinks that Bill is a perfect husband, except that he sometimes throws his coat on the floor when he comes home.

If I were worth 52 billion dollars and my wife started complaining about something like that, I'd be looking for the next Mrs. Wolfsie.

But when someone that successful has a bad habit, it's worth reconsidering your own lifestyle. Maybe Bill Gates knows something we mortals don't. Who knows from whence greatness originates? And who knew I'd be 55 years old before I ever used the word "whence"?

In this way, Bill Gates and I have a great deal in common. When I was single, I didn't have real strong feelings about what was on my floor. Or in my mouth or on my back, for that matter. So on any given day you could find on the floor a baseball mitt, an overcoat or an old salami sandwich. A floor is a good place to put stuff. Bill and I think alike.

And it's a great place to find stuff. There are no

hidden places on a floor. Things can't be shoved to the back of a floor. Floors are usually well lit. Things can't fall off of a floor and hit you on the head.

But ever since I was a kid, my mother would say: "Pick your coat up off the floor." When I got married, I heard the same thing from my wife: "Pick your coat up off the floor." Just for the record, I'm not worth $52 billion. And I think it might be the same coat.

I have never been a big fan of closets. They are poorly lit, difficult to maneuver in and often foul smelling. When I was in elementary school, we had something called a cloak room, which turned out to be a place where I went to take off my galoshes and get smacked around by the sixth grade bully. I'm still afraid that Georgie Lyons is in my hall closet. My wife is not sympathetic to this excuse. But again, I'm not worth 52 billion.

Closets are not very functional or efficient. You can search in a closet for your red down parka until you're blue in the face and never see it behind your wife's lime green windbreaker. You can take a search party into a closet to look for your Isotoner gloves and you'll never find them up on the top shelf of the closet behind the Scrabble game.

But throw your gortex boots and your earmuffs on the carpet next to your orange scarf and you'll find everything. Okay, maybe you'll trip over them. But, hey, there they are.

Yes, floors have it all over (and under) closets. There are floor walkers and floor planners and floor managers. There are no similar employment opportunities with closets. Tell *that* to Alan Greenspan.

And you can't clean a closet. No way. Let's see: There's floor wax and floor polish, right? Try to buy closet polish. They'll think you are from the *Third Rock from the Sun*.

That's all I have to say about floors and closets. I hope I beat Andy Rooney to it.

M.E.
and
ME

My wife, Mary Ellen, has a wonderful sense of humor. She has read every one of these essays, many of which make fun of her, and she has not said a word.

It's been a year now. I hope she will talk to me soon.

Three Kind Mice

I think I should be honest and tell you that we have mice. Last summer, my wife and I had come to the realization that we had woodpeckers. But there's a big difference between having mice and having woodpeckers. Having woodpeckers is something you can mention at a cocktail party and someday those very same people will flock to your back yard for a flank steak cookout or sit in your kitchen and gorge themselves on your homemade avocado dip. The fact that you have woodpeckers does not diminish your stature in the community one bit or call into question your worthiness as a neighbor. This is not true of mice.

In fact, after news got out about the woodpeckers, several people called with advice. There was even some suggestion that I simply tolerate the pecking. One neighbor told me that killing a woodpecker was a federal crime. A few folks actually came over with beer to see and hear the birds at work. What I thought was a real problem, made me the talk of the neighborhood...

"Say, did you hear that Dick Wolfsie has wood-peckers?"

"No, is that right? Well, leave it to an Easterner like Dick, a man of the arts, to do something classy and dramatic."

This is not the same reaction you get when word leaks out you have mice.

"Have you heard that Dick Wolfsie has mice?"

"You're surprised? He's from New York. And he's in television. You don't have to be Kreskin to predict this."

Before I go any further, let me be honest and tell you that I'm not sure we have mice. I am sure we have a mouse. Despite my wife's insistence that we are infested with the creatures, I believe it is the same mouse every time. Debating this point has become almost surreal...

"Dick, I think it's several different mice. The first one seems nervous and shy. This other one is aggressive and quick. And there's this one under the kitchen sink that just seems lost."

"Mary Ellen, please don't do this. The more you assign these rodents a personality, the more difficult it is going to be to get rid of them."

"What do you mean by 'get rid of them'? Look, Dick, I want you to get rid of the mice, but I don't want you to ever tell me you got rid of them. I do not want any information about this. I hope this is clear."

"You don't want any specifics on how they died?"

"Do NOT mention the word 'die' in this house. Go on the computer, Mr. Internet, and see if there's some catch and release program you can take a course in. Maybe there is a mice relocation project. I do not want to hear about how any mouse succumbed to some sick, barbaric trap that you bought at the hardware store. And you be nice to Seymour. That's the little nervous guy under the sink."

"Mary Ellen, please don't give them names. This is just making it worse when I have to... well, you know..."

"Too much information! Too much information!"

So there you have it. After watching *The Sopranos* for just one year on HBO, Mary Ellen had become the supreme don, dispensing the ultimate punishment with the wave of her hand, but opting to be left totally ignorant of the details.

Well, I accomplished my goal and I will spare you any specifics, but my wife wanted to know if I had been successful. It was just a week or so ago that she posed the question...

"Dick, I have a question for you and I expect complete candor, totally devoid of any details. There can be no indication in your answer that any violent act has ever occurred in this home that I could remotely feel guilty about. Okay, here I go. Be gentle. Have you taken care of the mouse problem?

"Mary Ellen, are you familiar with the famous poem, "The Night Before Christmas?"

"Yes, and you needn't say another word. You're not half the rat I thought you were."

Fast Walking Girl

My wife walks faster than I do. I had never thought much about this before, but I guess I've always kind of known it. Come to think of it, if I hadn't broken into a full gallop down the aisle the day we got married, she'd have beaten me to the justice of the peace by a nose.

It seems odd that I'm bothered by this at my age, but there's a certain demeaning aspect to this whole unpleasant issue. For example, when we take a walk around the block, Mary Ellen has to turn around every three or four minutes and walk back around me so that she doesn't get too far ahead.

As embarrassing as this is, I demand that she do it because a 55-year-old man should not be yelling to his wife, "Wait up!," an expression that I thought I had stopped using in junior high school back in New York.

What makes this more humiliating is that I have always been a good athlete. I played center field on my high school baseball team and even ran track one year. My wife is not really an athlete and never claimed to be. When my wife tries to run, she doesn't bend her legs at the knees and she ends up looking like a soldier doing a goose-step on too much coffee.

No, she can't run. But boy can she walk.

And I can't figure out why she walks faster. Let's see…her legs are longer than mine. And wait, she moves them back and forth faster than I do. Okay, I just figured it out. But this doesn't make me feel any better.

The great irony in this is that one of the reasons I was attracted to my wife 22 years ago was her long, slender legs. This is exactly how men get themselves in trouble. When I saw those lovely limbs, my mind turned to romance, but I should have realized that she'd be walking faster than me for the next 40 years. I knew I was going to marry a woman who was smarter. But faster? That wasn't the plan.

In fact, in high school and college, I prided myself on my speed. One thing was sure: I never had anything to do with girls who were fast.

I probably should rewrite that sentence, but I'm on a deadline.

Now, I must admit that when I walk my dog, Barney, he also walks faster than I do. This is a bit rough on the ego because Barney is 88 in dog years, 10 pounds overweight, and has arthritis. But the difference between Barney and my wife is that Barney actually turns around every few minutes to be sure I haven't had a coronary. I've considered using a leash, but neither of them likes the idea.

Sometimes, just to feel loved and wanted, I hide behind a tree to see if my wife will look for me. Out on a hiking trail, this is okay, but in a residential neighborhood, men behind trees are frowned upon. When you are telling your story to a police officer and he keeps using the word "lurking," you have a great deal of explaining to do.

The result, of course, is that I no longer take walks with my wife. She feels like I slow her down and the sight of her circling me every few minutes has the neighbors talking. Instead, when my wife and I want to walk, we go in different directions around our neighborhood circle. No matter how leisurely I walk, we pass each other at exactly the same time.

I know that was an incredibly stupid thing to say. But don't try to explain it to me. You know how slow I am.

Sit Down Lunch!

My wife has decided to make a career change. This change will bring my wife back into our home during the day while she looks at some potential opportunities. I work from home as well, and for 20 years I have ruled the roost. It is easy to be the roost ruler when there is only one rooster. That may change.

"Dick, I hope you don't mind, but we will have to share the computer."

"Not a problem, Dear. Sharing is what marriage is all about."

"And the fax machine."

"What's mine is yours."

"And I'll probably be on the phone quite a bit."

"Go for it. I want this to be as easy on you as possible."

"Oh, this will be so much fun. And we can have lunch together at home."

Suddenly, the blood drained out of my head. I started to perspire. A twitch developed in my right eye and I doubled over in pain. If I weren't careful, she'd know I was not happy with that suggestion.

How do you tell someone after 20 years that you really don't want to have lunch? You see, I've eaten lunch at home alone for over 10 years. When you are a man and you eat alone, you develop a few habits that will be hard to break. And my wife, who shares a significant DNA strain with Emily Post, would never understand. Maybe you will.

I know my wife. She'll want to have lunch around noon. I usually sit down to lunch sometime between 10:30 and 4:15. Boy is that a lie. I have never actually sat down for lunch in 10 years. I make the sandwich while standing at the fridge, then put it in my hand and eat it on the way upstairs to turn on CNN. I like this system. I have no plate to wash, no fork to rinse and by the time I get upstairs, I'm pretty much done eating and I can get back to work.

I just know that Mary Ellen is going to actually want to sit. Like at a real table. And then, I can just see it coming, we'll have to use utensils, like forks and spoons. When you eat lunch alone for 10 years, and no one is watching you, you slip into some pretty efficient habits. My wife would call them disgusting, but that's the Emily Post in her.

The more I think about this, the scarier it gets. And I even have nightmares about it. Sometimes I wake up screaming. I'm sitting at the kitchen table. Yes, sitting. And my wife has just asked me what we should do for a green vegetable. I know this doesn't sound like much of a nightmare, but even I can't walk up a flight of stairs and eat spinach without a plate and a fork. Heaven knows, I've tried.

Wait—the nightmare continues. She'll want to have conversation. I love my wife; I love to talk to her. But not in the daylight. Not during the week. Conversations are okay at dinners. So are utensils and chairs. But not at lunch. Not after 10 years.

It gets worse. She'll want to clean up before we eat. You know, put everything away. I can't eat that way. When I make a BLT, I leave the mayonnaise out for several hours. Then, five minutes before my wife gets home from work, I stick it back in the fridge. Has it turned bad? Will I poison the entire family? I don't know. But it's the only excitement I have all day.

And here's the kicker: In the nightmare, my wife enters the kitchen and sits down next to me. And then she says: "I can't believe you are wearing sweats and a dirty T-shirt. You should be embarrassed to sit down for lunch looking like that."

So the rest of the nightmare I'm allowed to stand up. Eating my lunch. Just like the old days.

It was a dream come true.

Rash Behavior

My wife has poison ivy. And she's got it bad. We're not sure how she got it. Maybe our cats or Barney got it in the woods and then snuggled up next to my wife in bed. Maybe I got it working in the back yard and then transmitted it to my wife when we were snuggling up in bed. One thing is sure: the amount of snuggling in my house has been cut back considerably this week.

You learn a lot about a relationship when your wife (or husband) breaks out in a rash. My wife has pretty good skin. In her entire life she's only had two pimples—the nights of the junior and the senior proms—so getting a bad case of poison ivy was kind of a bummer.

Most women would not see a case of poison ivy as a chance to test my love and commitment. But Mary Ellen never passes up a golden opportunity. Keep in mind that I had already gone out during the U.S. Open Golf Tournament to get her a topical ointment at the pharmacy. What greater demonstration of devotion is there? (I'm not bragging, but when I care for a woman, I'm about as selfless as a guy can get. I once dated a girl who needed insulin during *Monday Night Football*. Soon as half time came, I was on it.)

Meanwhile, the poison ivy got worse and worse. By Saturday night, poor Mary Ellen was in a great deal of discomfort, but not enough to let an opportunity pass...

"Do you still love me when I look like this?"

"Why in heaven's name would you ask me that?"

"Well, you just went out and played three sets of tennis with Cliff. You hate tennis. And you hate Cliff."

"This is silly, Mary Ellen. Wouldn't you love me if I got fat and lost my hair?"

"I've already proven that."

"Very funny. Look, I'm not embarrassed to admit that a certain percentage of my love for you is based on physical attraction."

"What percentage?"

"Oh, gosh. That's hard to say. Less than 100%, I can tell you that."

"Suppose, just suppose, Dick, that you found out I was going to look like this forever? How would that affect our lives?"

"I don't know, but it would certainly have an impact on Cliff's life."

"You're making a joke about this, and I'm serious. I want you to look me in the eye and tell me you'll love me no matter how I look."

"I'm having a lot of trouble just locating your eyes."

"You have one more chance to dig yourself out of this hole."

"Let me say this, Mary Ellen. No matter how many red, disgusting blotches you have on your face, anyone can tell how beautiful you were...are. I mean are... how beautiful you are."

By Sunday morning Mary Ellen was looking 100% better so I decided that if I showed her some affection I'd be forgiven...

"Well, Dick. You're being very attentive this morning. Are you itching for a little romance?"

"I am."

"Have you got that little compulsive list you make out every morning with everything you're going to accomplish during the day?"

"Yes."

"Scratch me off it."

Packing It In

It was the night before we were to leave for Alaska and I figured I'd better start packing. I'd been putting this off as long as I possibly could because packing is my least favorite part of a trip. Here are a few things I'd rather do than pack: get on the wrong plane; lose my passport in a non-English-speaking country; drink suspicious looking water; discover that my baked chicken was really monkey.

But pack I must. And so must my wife, Mary Ellen. It would be easy to make fun of her—you know, make a big deal about how much stuff she takes. But that would mean making up a story just to get a cheap laugh. You know I would never do that.

The truth is that Mary Ellen does something before she packs that drives me crazy: She actually thinks about it. You can understand why this bothers me. It's like going food shopping and making a list. Or putting things back where they belong. Or not over-ordering at a restaurant. It's like putting the tops back on food containers. Talk about taking the real joy out of life's pleasurable experiences.

Let me explain what my wife does. You tell me if this isn't a downer:

Before packing, she takes into account stuff like climate. Then she looks at the itinerary to see how many evenings will require formal clothing. Then she mixes and matches various outfits so she can dress differently each day, but pack fewer things. Then—oh this will just kill you—she thinks about how to actually put this stuff in the suitcase so it takes up less room. I love her to death, but is this annoying, or what?!

I have a different approach. I buy suitcases about the same size as my bureau drawers. For every day we're gone, I throw in a drawer. This system has never failed. True, one time in Bermuda, I had 50 pairs of socks, four wool sweaters and one pair of underwear, but I'm always on the lookout for conversation starters.

Most men never learn to pack. Men learn to throw a football, hit a wedge shot, fly fish, even cook an omelet. But no self-respecting man would put down his Budweiser to learn the fine nuances of packing. When I was a kid, I watched my grandmother stuff a turkey. That was good enough for me. The test of intelligence is the application of one learning experience to a variety of situations. Enough said!

I don't know where my wife learned to pack, but I have a theory…

"Mary Ellen, what's that you're putting in the suitcase?"

"Oh, it's a little plastic baggy filled with a touch of

olive oil, a book of matches and a moth ball. It's supposed to keep your pantyhose from drying out."

"That is the most ridiculous thing I have ever heard."

"This is so you. It's bad enough you scoff at Dear Abby's advice. Now you question Heloise. Are there any of the Ten Commandments you want to take issue with?"

"Any other tips?"

"Here are a few of my own: Line the suitcase with garbage bags to keep out moisture; use tennis ball containers for toiletries and pack half your clothes in the other spouse's suitcase, in case one bag is lost."

"Hey, those are great ideas, Mary Ellen."

"Yes, in fact I'm thinking of writing a book. Maybe I'll call it *Mary Ellen's Helpful Hints*. What could I get for a book like that?"

"Probably a nice lawsuit."

That's the
Ticket

My wife was pulled over by the police this past
weekend. Mary Ellen is a very law-abiding citizen. But
when she decides to challenge authority, she generally does it during a holiday season. She's always had a
flair for the dramatic.

Quite frankly, my wife is the most honest person I
have ever met. My own honesty is a bit questionable,
which kind of makes you wonder just how true that
statement about my wife is. I don't want to get side-
tracked, but in a college philosophy class 30 years
ago, a little conundrum like that one put me in therapy for almost two months.

Yes, my wife is honest. Too honest. Mary Ellen, for
example, believes rules were made to be followed.
This kind of harebrained notion is causing a rift in the
way we are raising our son. Now, I am not a crook,
(they don't call me Tricky Dick for nothing), but if my
wife were a judge presiding over some of my behav-
ior, I'd be in the slammer the rest of my life.

That's why getting stopped by the police has crushed her, ruined her perfect record and pretty much put a damper on the new millennium. My wife's life was exemplary. She never stayed after school, never cheated on a test, never pushed into line, never told a lie, never even hot-wired a car. The woman was a saint. Until Saturday, that is.

When you have a perfect record—not just in driving, but in your entire life—being followed by a police officer is a perplexing experience. I have studied several psychological extracts on the best way to deal with the fuzz when they pull you over. I know statistically the best things to say and not say. I know, for example, that saying, "Officer, I was running out of gas, so I had to get home quicker," just doesn't work. Do your research. It pays off.

Mary Ellen, on the other hand, has no experience in this area. When she noticed the lights flashing behind her, she waved the policeman around her. In fact, she waved him around her for about 42 blocks. Then it dawned on her that he was after her.

"May I see your license and registration, Ma'am?"

"Oh, there must be some mistake, Officer. I've never done anything wrong in my entire saintly life. I think you must have me confused with my husband."

"Look, Lady, I have to go back to the patrol car and check your record."

"While you're checking my record you might take notice of the fact that I have never cheated on a test, from kindergarten through my MBA. And this is especially noteworthy: I never let anyone look at my paper, either."

"Ma'am, your license plates are expired."

"How could I possibly know that?"

"There's a little sticker on the plate. It's last year's."

"Well, how can you expect me to see that from here?"

I actually tried that line once hoping to get a laugh from a policeman. I got a sobriety test instead. When my wife returned home, she was very upset.

"Dick, I was pulled over by the police today."

"Don't you just hate it when a heist goes bust?"

"Look, this is not a joke. Up until Saturday at noon, I had a perfect record. I had never done any-thing wrong in my life. Do you know what this stain on my reputation means?"

"A big celebration at the convent! You've moved a lot of the sisters into first place."

This entire event apparently created some soul searching on my Mary Ellen's part...

"You know, Dick, this brush with the law has given me a new perspective. I've led too sheltered an existence. In fact, marrying you is really the only really shady, questionable thing I've done in my life."

"Mary Ellen, marrying me was not exactly com-mitting a crime."

"No, but it's probably the closest I'll ever come."

Pecking Orders

The other day my wife called me from her office. Mary Ellen seldom calls to just chat. Usually it's something that requires my immediate attention—something only a man can handle. Something that will reinfuse me with a sense of my own masculinity.

"Dick, one of the tires on my car needs air."

"Really? And I have three pencils here that need sharpening." (This is the kind of banter that has led our close friends to label us soulmates.)

"I need you to come over to my office and deal with this."

"Mary Ellen, I don't know why you can't take care of this yourself. If I come over, I have to first drive to your office, leave my car, take your car to the service station, return your car, then get mine and drive it home."

"Heavens! I had no idea getting air in a tire was so complicated."

It's this kind of response that usually leads me to take the dog for a long walk while I ponder the many layers of that remark. Then I usually return home and slam my head against the aluminum siding. I continued: "It's not complicated. It's very easy. What's complicated is that you want me to do it for you."

"Well, isn't that just like you to make things more difficult?"

"Mary Ellen, I find that statement very frustrating."

"Well, Barney can use another walk. Or do you want to go directly to head slamming?"

When I reached the office, my wife was waiting for me outside.

"Dick, I know you are in a rush, so I'll go with you and help."

"Help me? You can't help me. I'm putting air in a tire. That requires one person, one hose, one tire. How could you possibly help me?"

"If this is any indication of your Christmas spirit, it's going to be a long December. Okay, do it yourself. Or would you rather call someone?"

And there's the expression that drives me up the wall. When she says, "Can you call someone?" the actual translation is: "I want this done right; you will mess it up; it will cost us more money; find someone who knows what he's doing."

As you can now see, Mary Ellen has absolutely no respect for my "fix-it" abilities, but she does have tremendous faith in my Rolodex. She is convinced that while I am personally inept, I know everyone in Indianapolis because of my TV and radio shows.

"Dick, I'm off to work. There are woodpeckers pecking on the side of the house. Call someone and get them to stop. See you at dinner. Have a great day."

"Wait a second, I don't know anyone who knows how to stop woodpeckers from pecking."

"Don't be silly. You know everyone. Don't you know someone who has 2700 ceramic frogs in his house?"

"Yes."

"And don't you know a reptile ob-gyn?"

"Two of them."

"And don't you know someone who collects man-hole covers?"

"Three thousand of them. What a nice lady."

"And I bet you know someone who eats earthworms for their daily diet."

"Actually, I'm friends with the entire family."

"So, Dick, can you see why it's hard to believe that you do not know someone who knows how to stop woodpeckers from pecking the side of a house?"

She had a point. Over the years, I've probably met just about every off-beat person in central Indiana, but the woodpecker problem had me stumped. *(Actually, being "stumped" is more of a beaver problem.)*

I began my search, but with no luck. Well, almost no luck. As I made my way through the Rolodex, I finally reached the W's. And there it was, staring me in the face. A very old card with the name Woody. Just Woody. No last name. I racked my brains. Could it possibly be? I crossed my fingers and started to dial...

Honey-Do Felon

I think she did it, but I can't prove it. I know it was a purposeful act. She did it with the intent to deceive. I'm not sure how this will change our relationship. I do know that I will never be able to get a good night's rest again.

My wife added something to my TO DO list. And she did it while I was sleeping.

I take great pride in this list, as most men do. I have no fancy Palm Pilot, but each night I carefully make a list, meticulously numbered, containing all my obligations for the next day. Nothing is left out. A small circle sits before each obligation, just begging to be filled in. My every movement for the day is carefully noted and arranged in a chronological and geographical fashion on a mini legal pad so as to minimize excess driving. I give great thought to this to save time and gas. The list is, quite frankly, a work of art.

But I knew something was amiss last Thursday when I left Kokomo, Indiana, after a meeting, and drove home to Indy to change a light bulb on the front porch before I headed back to Kokomo to drop off a video tape. After dropping off the tape in Kokomo, I headed back to Indy to change the kitty litter. Then it was back to Kokomo for lunch.

I was starting to suspect something.

"Mary Ellen, have you done anything lately behind my back?"

"A bright guy like you? I'd never get away with it."

She had a point. Nevertheless, I had just driven 190 miles to clean a cat box and change a light bulb, so I was in no position to dwell in the intellectual limelight.

My wife does have unique ways of getting me to do chores. For some reason she resists coming right out and asking. Instead, she resorts to trickery and skullduggery.

"Dick, you know those Pacers play-off tickets? I think they flew up on the roof. I'm sure you'll find them while you're cleaning out the gutters." I mean, how dumb do I look? It only took me three seasons to catch on to this little game.

Sometimes she leaves me little notes on my bathroom mirror. "Dick, you great big handsome guy, who I can't live without and whose very existence excites me, please unclog my shower drain."

It took me a while to figure this one out. Then I realized my wife always found me more alluring immediately after she washed her hair. I wasn't born yesterday, you know.

And then there was the time I accidentally overheard her talking very loudly on the phone to her friend, Pat...

"Pat, this will be such a great birthday surprise for Dick. I just hope all his friends flying in from all over the country don't trip on that broken step on the front porch."

The next day I fixed the step. My birthday was three months ago, and still no party. This was a bigger surprise than I thought. I finally laid down the law.

"Mary Ellen, I'm tired of all this chicanery. We are going to start a new system. If you want me to do a chore, you just come right out and ask me. That kind of communication makes for a healthy marriage. Is that a deal?"

"It's a deal. Now could you please clean up the storeroom downstairs?"

"Not this weekend. I have a big golf match."

"Could you fix the screen door?"

"Sorry, I'm too tired."

"Well, could you clean the fireplace?"

"I don't want to get that dirty."

"Dick, I haven't gotten you to do one chore. This new system of yours doesn't work."

"Works for me."

Refusing to Budget

My wife has decided that we need to go on a budget. I've told her that I would cooperate, that budgets are essential to good financial planning. In these economic times, a budget is crucial to the survival of a family.

I don't believe a word of it.

A budget is like a diet. Seems like a good idea, looks great on paper, and has a nice sound to it. I mean, can you make up three dumber reasons to do something?

Yes, I have always told my wife that budgets are a good idea. But this time, she's serious about actually doing this, which changes everything.

When we first got married, Mary Ellen toyed with the idea of a budget, but when she realized that saving money required not spending as much, the idea lost a bit of its glow. My wife now has an MBA, which has given her a new appreciation for some of the nuances of fiscal planning.

She will be very meticulous about this. She'll want receipts; she'll question each expense; everything will be scrutinized. I'd leave home, but I just know there will be no moving expenses in this budget.

"I'm dreading this, but let's get started."

"Okay, Dick, let's begin by each of us naming expenses that we have every month and that we can't change. Then we will know what our basic, fixed expenses are."

"Okay, Mary Ellen, I'll say the mortgage."

"Panty hose."

"The car payment."

"Make-up."

"Gas and electricity."

"Hairdresser."

"You know, Mary Ellen, I don't think you're really into the spirit of this. The car payment is a very different category than make-up and panty hose."

"Would you want to sit next to me in the car with bad hair and no make-up?"

"Point well taken. Let's go on."

"Okay, Dick. Now we'll each name something that we think the other person could save on. For example, I think you should give up that cup of coffee and low-fat muffin you've eaten every day on the way to work for 20 years."

"Why would I do that?"

"According to an article I read in *Money* magazine, if we had saved that four dollars a day for two decades, invested it in IBM, Intel, Amazon.com and Yahoo, then sold all that stock before October of

2000, we'd be twelve million dollars richer. I bet that puts a little crimp in your caffeine addiction."

"I feel so selfish. Just think, if I had not gone to Starbucks instead of not going to Village Pantry, we'd be billionaires."

"Here's another way we can save, Dick. Beginning today, we are going to start to make sacrifices. We will save by changing the oil in the car ourselves; we will save by doing the lawn work ourselves; we will save by cleaning out the gutters ourselves; and we will save by washing the car ourselves. I certainly hope you know the meaning of the word 'save.'"

"Mary Ellen, I certainly hope you know the meaning of the word 'we.'"

"Now we need to find a way to cut down on your office expenses."

"This is going to drive me to drink, Mary Ellen."

"Not a problem. Just be sure to turn in your mileage at the end of the month."

Cutting Remarks

I was thinking the other day about all the women in my neighborhood who mow their lawns. My wife doesn't mow our lawn. She has never mowed our lawn. I don't think she will ever mow the lawn. Lawn mowing season is right around the corner and it just kinda drives me crazy trying to figure out why she won't mow the lawn.

I want to ask her about this, but I am afraid that she'll assume I want her to mow the lawn. This couldn't be farther from the truth. If she started mowing the lawn, that would jeopardize our relationship by altering the delicate balance between my wife's independence, her femininity, and her sexuality.

Of course, if she really wanted to mow the lawn, I wouldn't stop her.

Don't misunderstand. I am not accusing my wife of being lazy. She works very hard outside the home as a hospital administrator, she spends endless hours working with my son on his schoolwork and still finds the time to whip up an occasional tasty meal.

I'm just really curious why she won't mow the lawn.

When I decided to marry Mary Ellen, I guess it didn't matter. I mean, after all, she was intelligent, beautiful, sensitive and caring. It was all a man could want.

I guess I just assumed that if push came to shove, she'd mow the lawn. Read that last sentence again...very funny!!

Of course, when we first got married, we lived in an apartment and she really had no opportunity to hone this skill—and you don't see a lot of lawn-mowing women in apartments. Then we moved to a condo and again there were few really good role models for her.

Not that I really care, but I bet if I threw my back out and the grass got really tall, she'd mow then.

When we moved to our first house, the lawn was pretty big and that's when our son was born, so I guess expecting her to mow and bottle feed at the same time would have been asking too much.

Sometimes I watch those other women mowing and I actually find it kind of unattractive. I mean, they're wearing old, ratty slacks and sweating pro-fusely and it's the last thing I'd want my wife doing.

Of course, I wouldn't have to watch. And when she finished, she could just freshen up.

There are some days, of course, especially in the

summer, when I'd like to just sit on a lounge chair and sip lemonade, but instead I have to mow the lawn. That's where a wife who's willing to mow comes in really handy.

I actually think it's kind of chauvinistic for a man to make his wife mow the lawn. Of course, on the other hand, it's kind of chauvinistic for a man to assume that a woman can't or won't mow the lawn, so I guess I should at least ask her.

Maybe she really wants to, but is afraid I won't let her. I'm sure that's it.

Of course, mowing the lawn is not that easy. Lots of people think you just push this machine and voila!, the lawn is mowed. Lawn mowing requires a little planning, an effective technique, and some dedication.

My wife is capable of all that. I wonder what the problem is.

And those new mowers kind of guide themselves. They require very little strength. I'm sure that if she just knew the state-of-the art technology available, she'd jump at the chance to mow the lawn.

What's wrong with her anyway?

Maybe this is some passive-aggressive way of telling me that she doesn't love me anymore.

My friend, Jeff—his wife mows the lawn. He was over the other day and asked me why my wife never mows the lawn. I was as honest with him as I could be...

"I don't know, Jeff. I never really thought about it."

More Cutting Remarks

People frequently ask me if it bothers my lovely wife, Mary Ellen, that I write about her in my column. In fact, Mary Ellen is often asked the identical question. Well, not exactly identical. It's more like: "Why don't you divorce the lout?" By the way, I don't consider that a question. It's more like a suggestion. And I wish my mother would knock it off.

Mary Ellen is insightful enough to know that most of my columns are really poking fun at myself. Let's take last week, for example. No, that's not a good example. But recently I did gently chide my spouse in this column for refusing to mow the lawn. And she didn't like it one bit.

"Let me ask you a question, Dick. Which is better, not mowing the lawn, or doing a lousy job of it?"

Now, I'm no Rhodes scholar, but this sounded like I was being set up. I treaded lightly...

"I'm sure, Mary Ellen, that if you wanted to mow the lawn, you'd do a fine job."

"I'm talking about you, Lawn Boy. You do the worst job. And then you write a column making fun of me. I should be writing a column about you and your lawn mowing. Here's what I'd say: Your rows aren't straight; you get bored and change directions; you leave grass clippings all over the garage and sidewalk; you cut the grass far too short; and then you trudge grass and mud into the house. Not only that, you don't put in the right mixture of gas and oil and I think you need a new spark plug. Now how does that make YOU feel?"

"A little emasculated."

"Which reminds me: The blades need sharpening, too."

"Anything else you'd write a column about?"

"How about the way you make a bed? Last night the sheets hung way over on one side, and the pillows were twisted in the pillowcase. And then you tucked the bedspread in."

"Wow, this is pretty brutal criticism coming from someone who slept 12 uninterrupted hours last night."

"You know, Dick, when we got married, your mother warned me you had very little experience in the bedroom, but that's not the kind of disappointment I expected."

"Don't stop now. You're on a roll. Remember, you'd have to write a column every week."

"Here's another column. You have no clue how to load the dishwasher. You don't scrape the food off; you put the glasses in upside down; you put the

Tupperware on the wrong level; and worst of all, you put the forks where the spoons should be and spoons where the forks should be."

"I must admit that's pretty serious. I can imagine the trauma, Mary Ellen, to discover that the fork you were using to eat your filet mignon was washed in the wrong compartment."

"Fine, Dick, make light of it. I thought you wanted to know what I'd write a column about. And I haven't even mentioned the frozen lemonade."

"How can you mess up frozen lemonade?"

"Well, at least we're asking the same question. The directions say add four and one-quarter cans of water. I've been drinking your lemonade for 20 years. Look me in the eye and tell me how much water you've been adding."

"I can't tell a lie. Four cans. Just four cans. I rounded off to the nearest can."

"Why?"

"You know, this is just one of those things I'm not comfortable talking about."

Well, folks, next week my wife wants to write a column about me. I hope it's the part about me being inexperienced in the bedroom. I don't think I could bear the embarrassment of exposing the lemonade story.

Return Engagement

This is a time of great planning in the Wolfsie household. It's a week or two after Christmas. Calendars are being checked, appointment books logged, traffic patterns analyzed. The big question is: Have I waited long enough to return that horrible Christmas gift? My wife usually waits at least two weeks. She used to run back to the store at 7 a.m. the next day. This suggests to the giver that not only is the gift ill-conceived, but that the receiver would rather not spend any more time under the same roof.

My wife is usually pretty good at hiding her disappointment. Sometimes the only clue I have that she is unhappy with a gift is the widening of her eyes, the violent head shaking, finger down her throat, and the dropping of her jaw. Funny, I thought monogrammed Tupperware was a nice touch.

I used to think only men had problems finding

the perfect gift. But this past Christmas my wife started using an expression I have always dreaded:

"Dick, you are so hard to shop for."

Everyone in my family has said this to me. My brother, my sister, even my mother...

"Dick, you are so hard to shop for."

This was very difficult for a seven-year-old to take. My therapist thinks that my feelings of rejection, alienation, and depression may be related to this. Well, that's what he used to think. Then he saw me on television.

My wife usually starts getting frustrated right after the Fourth of July, already annoyed at me for being uncooperative. So last month the questions started.

"This year, Dick, I want to know exactly what you want for Christmas. And I want to know it before the first hard frost."

"Mary Ellen, you know it's no fun when I tell you."

"Okay then, I'm going to surprise you."

"I hate surprises."

"Fine, how about gloves or a new sweater?"

"You know I don't like to get clothing."

"Maybe a Palm Pilot or a cell phone with e-mail?"

"Please don't buy me gadgets. I can never work them."

"Books or tapes? You love those, Dick."

"No. I need to pick those out on my own."

"Gift certificates?"

"Fine, if you want to take the easy, insensitive way out."

"Dick, you are the most frustrating, ungrateful man I have ever met."

"Wow, what happened to your Christmas spirit?"

I guess I *am* hard to shop for. Last year, everything my wife bought me, I returned. Come to think of it, everything I bought my wife, she returned. Now, I'm not the smartest guy in the world, but I do see a pattern here that could save a lot of time and money. But Mary Ellen says this is all my fault. She claims I could be a better shopper if I just paid attention.

"Your problem is that you can't take a hint. I hint about what I want. But you're so dense. You never pick up on the hint."

"One example, please."

"Let's see. This year I casually mentioned that it would be fun if I could get into my pajamas at night and slip into bed with a laptop computer."

"I took the hint."

"No, Dick, I didn't want a new pair of pajamas."

"I thought you looked disappointed. Can you think of one more example?"

"Okay, for six months prior to our 20th wedding anniversary in June, I walked around the house humming "I Love Paris in the Springtime." I hummed it at breakfast, at dinner, in the shower. I hummed it in the car. What did you get me for our 20th anniversary?"

"The sheet music. I thought you'd get a kick out of knowing the lyrics."

Now that Christmas is over, I have to start worrying about my wife's birthday. But this time Mary Ellen is apparently trying to be even less subtle—if that's possible.

"Have you noticed some of the magazine pictures of women in gorgeous designer leather boots that I have casually left around the house, Dick?"

"Oh, you mean the photos taped to my bathroom mirror, my car's rearview mirror, the remote control and the one attached to my summer sausage in the fridge?"

"Yes, exactly. And what do you think will happen if you don't pick up on these clues?"

"I guess I'll be the one getting the boot."

Puzzling Behavior

When I got married in 1980, I was already an adult. I was 30-something and my wife was 20-something. I am still 30-something, but that "something" is now 25.

But I digress. When I said "I do," I knew about the responsibilities of marriage, the obligations and commitments I had to make. When I took the vow, I was ready to do anything to make our marriage work. Our marriage was based on honesty. We knew everything about each other. Almost.

Everyone has bad habits that he or she brings to a marriage. I don't wipe my feet, I drink out of the milk container, I leave the front door open, I lose tops to stuff in the fridge, I eat too quickly, I am a bit quick-tempered. Everyone has flaws. Mary Ellen knew mine.

There was one thing about Mary Ellen I didn't know.

In retrospect, I probably have a legal way out of

our marriage. I told my wife about all my former girlfriends; she knows that while in college, the campus police put me in the slammer for painting ELECT HUBERT HUMPHREY on the side of the girls' dorm; she even knows I was almost arrested in front of Shea Stadium in 1969 for an overzealous display of Mets fever. She knows all that.

But I never knew about her jigsaw puzzles. I first learned about my wife's obsession on our wedding night. Enough said. I was hoping it was the beginning of some erotic game that she read about in *Cosmopolitan*. At the very least, I thought the picture would reveal a man and woman in some R-rated embrace. At about 4 a.m. I realized it was a farm scene.

On our wedding night, Mary Ellen promised to teach me something new. I just didn't expect instruction on separating straight-edged pieces.

We've now been married for over 20 years and Mary Ellen, an MBA from the University of Michigan, an accomplished hospital administrator and an avid reader of the best seller list, is still obsessed with jigsaw puzzles.

I have trouble relating to this passion because when I tackle a project, the words "close enough" are usually heard at some point. This philosophy is somewhat abhorrent to the jigsaw puzzle maven who, for some inexplicable reason, expects every piece to fit perfectly. (Now what would Freud say about that?)

Mary Ellen has done scores of jigsaw puzzles since

we've been married. She approaches each puzzle in the same meticulous way, separating pieces by color and putting the straight edges in their own pile. Each color gets its own Tupperware container. She wears a brown bathrobe and blue slippers and eats Orville Redenbacher's popcorn. She works on the coffee table in the living room and watches a classic black and white movie on TV. Other than all that, she's pretty flexible.

When Christmases and birthdays arrive, buying her a jigsaw puzzle is a no-brainer. It's always appreciated. There was that one birthday when I had a graphics store make a 2000-piece puzzle of me in my boxer shorts. That's the only puzzle she's left unfinished.

But the problem with buying her a jigsaw puzzle is that the more pieces, the more complicated, and the better the chance that I'll be looking at that brown bathrobe all weekend. I've tried to lure her away.

"Mary Ellen, how about dinner at Ruth's Chris Steak House?"

"Love to—just 1200 more pieces to go."

"How long will that take?"

"Maybe a month. Go ahead and eat if you're hungry."

Right now, she's working on a huge puzzle with over 3000 pieces. She's been working on this puzzle since her birthday in May and it is causing a little stress in the family...

"Hey, Dad?"

"Yes, Brett?"

"You know, I've been watching Mom the last four months working on that puzzle every night, and I think I have a great idea for a birthday present that might brighten up all our lives up a bit."

"No! Not another puzzle."

"No, a new bathrobe."

Pet Peeves

I try to get most of my medical and health information from either *Good Morning, America* or *USA Today*. Relying too much on any one authority is risky, so I try to spread my intellectual net a little wider. I have found that Mondays are a particularly good day to find new medical research in the media. I think newspapers get the breaking, cutting-edge stories over the weekend because some researcher in Ontario, Canada, just can't look at another test tube and is already late for his 5:00 p.m. curling match, so he just calls *USA Today* and blurts out something like: Chocolate can reduce your blood pressure. Or: People who eat peanuts have fewer strokes. Well, that's pretty much all it takes, and the next thing you know, there isn't a Reese's Peanut Butter Cup between here and Lake County.

Lately, some of the research has been borderline *X-File* stuff. Last Monday's *USA Today* reported that nine hours' sleep is bad for you, but seven is good for you. How about eight hours? "It's neither good nor bad," said the researcher. Whatever that means.

"Dick, why are you setting your alarm for 6 a.m.? Tomorrow is Saturday."

"Well, Sweetheart, the paper said that sleeping nine hours is bad for your health. You live longer if you sleep seven hours."

"What will you do at 6:00 a.m. on a Saturday in the middle of winter?"

"Gee, I don't know—have a platter of bacon and eggs, then get up on the roof and clean out the gutters?"

This Monday's *Good Morning, America* was a real shocker. According to this researcher, most people with sleep problems are also people who snooze with their pets. The scientist believes that pets are responsible for their owners' insomnia.

Well, I was dumbstruck. I just don't want to hear anything negative about our dog and cats. Why, it was just last Saturday night, after getting up at 2:30 in the morning to let Barney out and then again at 3:00 a.m. to let the cat in, that I said to my wife—after taking the cat off her head so I could see her face—how much we love our animals. Imagine someone saying pets negatively affect our sleep habits!

The scientist went on to say one reason your pets are up all night is because they sleep during the day. It is amazing what a post-graduate degree will allow you to say with a straight face. So, this Ph.D. suggests people find activities during the day to keep their Dobermans, Labs and pit bulls intellectually stimulated so they don't nap in the middle of the afternoon.

I can't even keep myself that intellectually stimulated, so tell me how to make this work with an 11-year-old, fat beagle and two 20-year-old cats, one of which has not moved from the sofa in the living room in six years, except to come upstairs at night and sleep on my wife's face.

One suggestion was to feed the dog several times a day so that he is always alert and waiting for his food. I know this won't work, because on a typical Saturday afternoon, I eat about six times myself. Then I try to nap in between bites so I can always wake up to a snack.

I did try playing with the dog on the floor, but he fell asleep. Then I played with him on my bed, but I fell asleep. Then I put on the TV and turned to *Animal Planet*. We both fell asleep.

This was starting to really stress me out, but it was Thursday already and I was sure some scientist at the University of California was just about to release a new study saying animals have a calming influence on your life and will make you sleep better.

That will give me a little breathing room for a week.

Age-Old Humor

A chapter for those of you
who are getting older.
All others, please skip
this part and go on
to the next section.

Row V. Wade

The Wolfsies just got back from whitewater rafting in West Virginia, our last vacation of the summer, and we're awfully darn proud of ourselves. We are especially proud that despite the tension created by a 1200-mile car trip; despite the tension created when three people with totally different sleeping habits share a tiny hotel room; despite the tension created when all three people want to eat at a different restaurant every night; despite all this tension, we are still a nuclear family, to use Margaret Mead's term very loosely. We're just lucky the bomb didn't go off.

I'll admit I was a little uneasy about this trip. At the Boat Sport and Travel show last winter, I watched several videos of people whitewater rafting. It did look like fun. Everyone was laughing and giggling. But I still think that whenever you do something that requires a life vest AND an army helmet, there's something they're not telling you.

When we arrived in Fayetteville, West Virginia, we went directly to the cabin where we had reserved our rafting adventure. Whitewater rafting, we discovered, is divided into what are called levels. Level I is pretty much mildly choppy water and is for rafters with absolutely no experience and for people who have a good reason to get back home. At the other extreme is Level VI which is very dangerous and recommended for people who are either trapped in dead-end marriages or those diagnosed with terminal illnesses and given less than four hours to live.

Before they give you a paddle, the guides need to assess your experience with high adventure. I told the guide this was my first time.

"Are you serious, Mr. Wolfsie? You are 55 years old and you have no experience rafting?"

"Well, I'd hardly say NO experience. I mean, I have read *Huckleberry Finn* four times."

"Do you have any specific concerns, Mr. Wolfsie?"

"Is there any chance that the raft could turn over?"

"Gee, I can't even recall the last time that happened."

"That long ago, huh?"

"No, it's just that I've banged my head on rocks so often, I have no short-term memory."

Then they started asking about my physical ability to make the trip:

"Does anyone have a knee injury?

I quickly raised my hand.

"Yes, Mr. Wolfsie. Is your knee a problem?"

"Bad knee. Yes, I have a very bad knee. I've had

three arthroscopic surgeries. I have a withered anterior cruciate ligament coupled with progressive osteoporosis, severe arthritis, and degenerative cartilage, bruised tendons and decalcifying ligaments."

"Wow! Could your good knee support you in an emergency?"

"That IS my good knee."

I discussed my medical situation with the guide, focusing on my lower back problems and my pulled hamstring. When that didn't work, I launched into my high triglycerides and that pesky family history of bad HDL/LDL levels.

I couldn't squirm out of it. So we set out on the rapids. My wife was incredibly calm; my son remarkably in control and adept with the paddle. I felt as though I had picked up the Stepford Family at the lodge. Who were these people?

When we got home to Indianapolis, my wife and I watched the video of our trip ($69.95) and were both astonished to see just how nuts we were to do this. In the tape you see accomplished river guides being thrown 20 feet into the air and then sinking into the rapids. You see entire rafts capsizing and sinking into the raging river. Men and women are sucked into the white water, screaming as they disappear from sight.

"That couldn't possibly be us in that raft, could it, Mary Ellen?"

"It can't be. We'd never do anything that crazy. And you'd swear that's our son, Brett, next to those people who can't possibly be us. But it can't be our son, because we love him, and we are so overprotective that we would never take him on a ride like that. So it's probably just some other gorgeous 13-year-old."

I think that's pretty much the last time we'll go whitewater rafting. We have a lot of fond memories. But my son will never forget the trip. He still has the impression of all 10 of my fingers in his thigh.

Funny, I'm 55

I'm 55 now, and at that funny age. I think I should explain "funny." Funny can mean a number of different things. For example, a lot of people say to me, "Hey Dick, you are really funny." Well, maybe not a lot of people, but I think you get the drift. Sometimes, people will say, "This tastes funny." This has always struck me as odd, because when you think you're eating spoiled cottage cheese, it's hard to find something to chuckle about. Sometimes people use the word funny to denote a curiosity. You might hear someone say, "Funny, Ralph, I've known you for 20 years and never realized you only have one nostril."

So what does it mean to be at a funny age? Oh, I've been at funny ages before. Nine was pretty funny. Fourteen was a laugh riot. And 25 was just a 12-month grin. I could tell you more about 25, but this is a family book.

Of course, some ages are not the least bit funny. Sixteen, for example, was not funny—not for one second. And 40. You couldn't even get a smirk out of me. I think you get the point here. Some of you may even be finding this column funny—in a cottage cheese kind of way.

So why is 55 a funny age? Well, I just don't know where to put myself chrono-geriatrically. You see, I fought the term middle age for so many years that now that I am finally willing to accept it, it's too late. I got my AARP card in the mail special delivery about nine seconds after I turned 50. It had a few discount offers I could have taken advantage of, but that meant admitting I was 50. I think this is a major marketing problem for the folks over at Retirement Central. It's like giving 20% discounts for people who are lepers. There are just some discount cards people are hesitant to whip out in a movie line.

In my early 50s, I shunned the discounts, but now that I'm 55, some of the really good deals are about to kick in. I had a lot of pride up until about 53, but now two bucks off a movie is starting to sound pretty darn good.

Sixty is a good age, also. You enjoy some serious perks when you're 60. Sixty-two is also beneficial because retirement is an option. But never ever say you are in "your early sixties." Any time you preface your age with the word "early," you lose a lot of sympathy and several half-price coupons. Only say "early" when you're 21.

And then there's 65. This is the age when you should kick back and enjoy all the nifty financial inducements that are available to you. You may not get quite as many free admissions as you did when you were two years old, but at least you don't have to be accompanied by a parent.

The movie theater nearby gives discounts starting at age 60. I've been tempted to act a few years older with the hopes that they wouldn't check my ID. But here again, I can't win. If they do check my ID, I'll be exposed as the typical pre-penitentiary baby-boomer who is so materially oriented that he risks arrest and humiliation just to save two dollars at a 4 p.m. movie. On the other hand, if they don't check my ID because they think I really am 60, well you can be darn sure I'll never go to *that* movie theater again. I mean, if the kid selling tickets can't tell the difference between 55 and 60, who knows how many toddlers are walking into Madonna movies.

So there you have it. I'm 55 years old. Soon—God willing—I'll be 60. I think I'll celebrate by seeing a movie with my new discount. Then I'll take the two bucks I saved and go out for a nice cold beer. I can't think of anything better that could happen on my birthday.

Well, there is one thing: The bartender could check my ID.

Man from Nantucket

I recently returned from a vacation in Nantucket and I've decided that after 30 years in teaching, television, radio and newspapers, it's time for a low-pressure job.

I was considering Wal-Mart greeter. Very little stress there, but a friend told me that he once saw the Wal-Mart contract and there's an actual reference to being nice to people. Like I'd sign something like that.

Toll booth collector also seems pretty low stress. And it gives you a chance to meet lots of people without running the risk of ever establishing a real relationship. On second thought, that's too much like television.

Yes, I've thought a great deal about this. And I've made my decision. I'm going to be a tour bus driver. This is just too perfect. Here's why:

First of all, a tour bus driver doesn't really have to know anything. For example, our driver told us how Nantucket was founded when the Pilgrims came over and... no that's not it. Actually, the founding fathers were looking for a place for some R&R so they... no that doesn't sound right. It was actually the Puritans who were looking for cranberries... The point is that I really don't remember one thing she said, although at the time, I remember looking at my wife, raising my eyebrows and saying, "Wow, that's very interesting."

That's the great thing about being a tour bus driver. You can make up the wildest stories because people on a bus will believe anything and no one will remember it anyway. I love a job where there is no premium placed on the facts. My boss at Channel 8 gets real picky about this correctness thing. So do my newspaper editors. When I retire, I'm getting out of the accuracy rat race.

And even if you did remember what tour bus drivers told you, who would you tell? "EVERYBODY GATHER 'ROUND. I HAVE SOMETHING REALLY BIG TO TELL YOU ALL."

"Calm down, Dick. This must be really important to call a station meeting at 6 a.m."

"Are you ready? Listen to this: Hedge trimming is considered an art in Nantucket and—hold on to your seats—it dates back 1000 years."

Not exactly news you can use.

Another reason I'd be a great tour bus driver is that I have no sense of direction. Finally there's a job where I see no disadvantage in being geographically challenged. The people on the bus have no idea where they are going—that's why they took a bus. They know nothing about the area—that's why they need a tour guide. So when you're lost, you can make up some outrageous story about how it was in this very isolated area, hundreds of miles from food, water and medical treatment, that over 200 years ago three Catholic nuns saved the island of Nantucket by staying awake 72 straight hours to man the lighthouse with only dried cranberries to eat.

I told you I'd be good at this.

Most tour guides are retired from another job and many are grandparents. While I remember very little about the history of Nantucket, I do know from my trip that Adam is four and finally potty trained, and Erica is only two but talking up a streak. I don't think that most senior citizens really like driving a bus, but the lure of a microphone and a captive audience at 65 miles per hour is not something a doting grandparent can turn down.

I have other qualifications as well. I can drive a car Linda Blair-style with my head completely turned around. And most importantly, I can tell the same joke three times a day, 50 weeks a year, and still laugh at it.

Yes, I'm a natural for this line of work. I can't wait to start. See you on the bus.

Sleepless in Alaska

I can't sleep. It's midnight and I have to get up in three hours to go to work at Channel 8. That's why I am downstairs on the computer writing.

Sleeping has always been a problem for me. Not napping. I'm a wizard at napping. But sleeping. Like in my own bed. Like for six to eight hours. I'm just not very good at it. Never was.

No one sleeps better on a bus than I do. The second I get in the seat, I'm unconscious. But why is that? There is nothing on a bus that lends itself to sleeping. And yet, in 1988 Mary Ellen and I went to Europe and I slept through most of the NATO countries. In fact, we just got back from a vacation in Alaska where my mass transit sleeping rivaled some of the brown bears in hibernation.

In order to deal with my insomnia, I decided that I should try to simulate the very conditions on a bus that send me to never-never land.

One night I requested my wife stand at the foot of

the bed and talk about whaling in Juneau. In Alaska, when the bus driver started spouting off about whales (sorry!), I felt my eyes get heavy. I think Mary Ellen felt kind of dumb talking to me from the foot of the bed, but she did it. But then I asked her to rock the bed back and forth so I'd feel like I was on the bus. That was getting a little too kinky so she opted to sleep on the couch.

I was still wide awake, however, so I determined that it clearly wasn't the tour guide rap that made me sleepy. Next, instead of getting into bed, I took a hard-back chair and sat straight up in it. Then I bounced up and down like I was on a bus and looked sideways out my bedroom window. But I was still wide awake after 10 minutes. Then I figured maybe it was the sun that makes me drowsy so I shined a floor lamp directly in my eyes. Then I started bouncing up and down again. (I think my neighbor, Norm, could see me doing all this from his bedroom window, which might explain why he kept winking at me the next day when we played tennis.)

No luck. Still wide awake.

Then I had another idea, so I woke Mary Ellen and explained my new theory.

"No, Dick. You cannot invite 30 strangers over to the house to sit around you when you sleep."

Then it hit me. The bus trips are during the day, but I'm trying to sleep at night. So the next day, I got back into my chair at nigh noon, sat straight up, looking out my bedroom window.

Nope. Still wide awake.

Wait a second. The scenery wasn't changing. Maybe that's what lulls me to sleep. I started moving the chair from one window to the next. The sun was pouring in on my face. Suddenly I felt myself getting sleepy, very sleepy.

ZZZZZZZZZZZZZZZZZZZZ

It worked. I slept from noon until 8 p.m., sitting straight up in the chair, leaning against my bedroom window. My insomnia was cured.

At 10 p.m., two hours later, it was time for bed. I got under the covers and just couldn't fall asleep.

Go figure.

Sleepless in Indianapolis

My day begins at 3:30 a.m. I can't stay up very late at night because I have to get up so early in the morning in order to appear on Channel 8 by 5 a.m.

This situation has its drawbacks. For example, I'll start watching a sporting event and when I think things are pretty much over, I hit the sack and doze off to sleep. Then I wake up and find out that I missed a really close game. Things always seem to get really exciting when I get into bed. (Wow, I wish that were as good as it sounds.)

When you're a grown man and have to go to bed at 7 p.m., your life does take on some interesting twists. For example, I've always thought a father should kiss his son good night before bedtime. My wife agrees.

"Brett, go upstairs and kiss your dad good night."

"Gosh, Mom, do I have to? The six o'clock news is just getting interesting."

Quite frankly, I have never been much of a sleeper. I snore, I toss and turn, I talk in my sleep, I get up four or five times to either get a drink of water or go to the bathroom. Sometimes I'll awaken and watch TV for 15 minutes or read. I usually stash a salami sandwich under my pillow and eat it about 2 a.m. People ask me if all this bothers my wife. I don't think she knows about it. She keeps her door shut.

My sleeping habits do annoy Barney. Dogs are supposed to sleep about 18 hours a day, so when I drag his Beagle behind out of bed at 3:30 a.m., I usually get the soulful look of a hound about to call the PETA hotline. I used to feel guilty about this, until I saw his last contract with Channel 8. I shouldn't complain about the dog. He doesn't mind when I snore or read. And he's crazy about those salami sandwiches.

I should tell you that my job at Channel 8 did not really alter my existing sleeping habits. I am some-what of a workaholic so I have always enjoyed going to bed early.

"Dick, why are you up at 5:00 a.m. again?"

"This is a great time to get work done. No phone calls, no annoying kids to disturb me. You can real-ly accomplish something this time of day."

"This is ridiculous. You're eight years old. Go back to bed."

"Yes, Mom."

For most young men, going to college was license to stay up late and have a good time. At my frater-nity house, I would usually leave the festivities about 11 p.m., go back to my bedroom and sleep until 3 a.m. Then I'd return to the party refreshed. Coming out of my bedroom at three in the morning often left the impression I had gotten lucky. I once slept six uninterrupted hours during a wild Greek celebration. How lucky can you get?

My wife, I should mention, is on a different clock. Mary Ellen is not a morning person. Let me explain what "not a morning person" means. She has never seen the sun rise. Not being from Missouri, Mary Ellen accepts the existence of this natural phenomenon without ever witnessing it. I commend her for that. Trust is important. But ask her how the newspaper gets on our front step by six in the morning and she's not willing to jump to any conclusions.

Most of my friends think my lifestyle is for the birds (roosters, I guess). They want to sleep in every morning so they can dream about retiring in their 50s. I have no such fantasy. I retire early every night.

Retirement Island

I think the CBS network has taken the wrong approach to their show *SURVIVOR*. What happened to all that hyped marketing to the older generation? Oh sure, they did stick a couple of token 40-plus people in the middle of Australia so America could see that even a kangaroo has better posture than a baby boomer. But I'm not buying it. Or watching it.

I have a better idea for a program. I'll call it *RETIREMENT ISLAND*. There will be two teams, each having 10 people over the age of 50. No belt size for the men can be under 38 and the women have to sign an affidavit they have never had cosmetic surgery. Competitions will include events like power mall walking.

I have already picked my team from former associates. I look forward to seeing—and competing against—your team. Good luck! Here's my tribe:

HERB: Herb is a 57-year-old insurance salesman who missed the 60s because he was playing with his slide rule. Herb will do well at many of the cerebral competitions. The only drawback is that Herb is allergic to 300 different things. Herb was a senior at George Washington University when I was a freshman. He was assigned to me to help with my first year of college. It was hard to get close to Herb. I made him sneeze.

KIMBERLY: Kimberly is the oldest person in America with that name. I dated her in college. She was a member of a radical feminist group in the early 70s, but gave it all up to marry the first male dental hygienist in this country. Now at age 54, she's willing to live dangerously for a month as long as she can bring her floss.

HOWARD: Howard is a 62-year-old CPA. We used to live next door to each other when I was single. Howard has aged a bit. He is the only person on earth who couldn't recognize himself in his own college yearbook.

JUNE: June, age 65, will be the oldest person on my team. At age 61, she dumped her old man and married her strength coach. When I was 22, I dated June, who was then 34. June will have some great stories to tell around the campfire including the time she and I... come to think of it, maybe June is a bad choice.

BURT: Burt, 50, is my best friend. Sort of. He discovered Jerry Springer and made him a star. Burt is responsible for the notion that talk shows could pay people to pretend that they hate each other.

Burt is bitter now because reality TV has taken over and people will hate each other on their own.

ERIC: Eric was my roommate in college. He is 54 and the TV critic for the *New York Post*. Eric was an intellectual in college. He hated TV. I read his columns on the Internet. He still hates TV. I want Eric on the island because he is a neat freak and will keep the place clean. Thirty years ago that drove me crazy. You'll wish he were on your team.

MARC: Marc was the campus radical at George Washington University in 1968. He organized 50 students for a sit-in at the White House to protest the Vietnam War. He also organized hundreds of students to boycott classes and block professors from getting to class. Marc was arrested twice for drugs and once for carrying a weapon onto the grounds of the Supreme Court building. I tracked Marc down through the Internet, knowing he would be perfect for our team. I was right. He's the executive chef at the Marriott in Miami, Florida.

MAX: This is the only Max I've ever known in my life. He was crude, self-centered, and obnoxious. He stole my girlfriend in high school, cheated me out of 50 bucks and ratted on me in the fifth grade. I want Max on Retirement Island just so I can kick his butt off. I've waited 40 years for this.

MORGAN: Morgan is a 27-year-old personal trainer. That's all I know. I saw her once at the supermarket. WOW! Hey, ratings are ratings.

Auto Neurotic

I just got back from Ireland and I feel very close to the Irish people. They are warm, gracious, and friendly. But they drove me crazy. Actually, I drove myself. And that made me crazy.

For one week, I drove the "highways" of Ireland. I am now safe at home and, with help of several Valium, willing to talk about it. My wife, who sat on the passenger side, is doing well at the local stress center.

It all began when my wife and I (and our son, Brett) decided to drive the beautiful countryside at our own leisurely pace, rather than take a tour bus. Keep in mind that Ireland has hundreds of thousands of narrow two-lane highways where cars speed around hairpin turns at 60 miles per hour. Ireland has many roads where your car will be either inches from a stone wall or millimeters from an approaching semi. Ireland also has a million head of sheep that enjoy congregating on the roadway. Ireland has wet and slippery roads. And in Ireland you drive on the left side of the road.

Because of all of this, the car rental people require that you go through a rigorous and extensive training session before they will lease you a car.

"Would you be Mr. Wolfsie?"

"Yes, I be. I mean, yes, I am."

"Here are the keys. Drive on the left or you'll die. Good luck. Next."

In case you ever do go to Ireland, here's some driving information Hertz and Avis won't give you:

1. If you have an accident on most Irish roads, it will take two days for an ambulance to find you. Then it takes two more days to get back to the nearest hospital. There are only six ambulances in all of Ireland. They all carry their own tombstones.

2. If you are traveling on a two-lane highway and go over the centerline, you will hear that screech that every driver dreads: his wife screaming at the top of her lungs.

3. Street signs are totally useless. First the sign says: Killarney 10 kilometers. You drive for 20 minutes and the sign says: Killarney 25 kilometers. Two minutes later the next sign says: Killarney 5 kilometers. These signs are obviously for people herding sheep.

4. Your spouse, if sitting in the front passenger seat, will develop a twitch. Mary Ellen and I were

celebrating our 20th wedding anniversary but I had never, in all the years we have known each other, seen her lose total control of her facial muscles.

5. Gas stations are never self-serve. If you pull into an Irish gas station and try to pump your own fuel, they will think you are stealing gas. Other than that, Irish gas stations are pretty much the same as those here in the United States. Except, of course, for the Guinness on tap. (Just kidding.)

6. Sometimes you can ease the tension in the car by amusing your children. However, it's not easy making a 12-year-old laugh. Here's a foolproof suggestion. The Irish pronounce the word "forty" as though it were "farty." So, you might say things like: "We're farty kilometers from Dublin." This puts most adolescents in stitches. If that doesn't work, just add that you may need to stop for gas. Trust me. You'll be a laugh riot.

7. To avoid divorce, instruct your spouse NOT to make jokes about your driving. Driving on the left side of the road is stressful. You will not be amused by remarks like: "It was nice having a side-view mirror, even if it was only for a short time." Or, "Will they charge us to repaint the left side of the car?" Half the couples who drive themselves come back from a vacation in Ireland and get divorced. The other half are widowed.

8. And finally, when you return the car, don't whine about how stressful and unpleasant your driving experience was. Be a proud American. Tell them that you found the road trip exciting and invigorating. Tell them that you felt in control every second and that you look forward to your next adventure on the Irish highways. Then pay the deductible and be glad you're going home in one piece.

Hobby Hubby

At age 55, it's probably a little late to fret about this, but when I was a kid I didn't have any hobbies. Oh, I played sports and had a very active playground life, but things like stamps, coins and butterflies just never held much fascination for me. As I get older, I sort of wish I had developed a few side interests. You know, a few pastimes that I could cultivate since I received my first AARP card (which arrived 22 seconds after I turned 50). I would be very happy with anything from needlepoint to collecting political buttons. But my wife has a different idea.

Mary Ellen thinks that the Wolfsies need more adventuresome hobbies. Apparently, our subdivision garage sale and our multi-block pitch-in dinner have not caused the kind of adrenaline rush she had hoped for. I tried to cheer her up...

"But, Mary Ellen, we could go whitewater rafting."

"You don't get it, do you, Dick? We could go whitewater rafting, but we will not be whitewater rafters."

"Yikes, I never thought of it that way. But tell me one thing."

"Yes?"

"What's the difference?"

"Don't you see? We can a take a vacation to go whitewater rafting, but we won't be rafters; we'll be drifters—drifters looking for a real hobby. Sometimes I ask my friends at work, 'What do you do for excitement?' Some say they are skiers. Some say they are rock climbers. Some say they are spelunkers. We are not skiers, we are not rafters, we are not spelunkers, we are not rock climbers, we are not..."

"We are not bungee jumpers."

"Exactly. I'm not used to your catching on."

This conversation started to depress me. My wife was right. I play tennis, but I am certainly not a tennis player. I play pool, but you'd hardly say I was a pool player. I even play cards, but... well, I think you get the point.

No different for Mary Ellen. She once baked some bread, but she's no baker. She runs to the supermarket, but she's no runner. She rides her bike, but no biker, she. *(Wow, I've been waiting to use that construction for 40 years.)*

So what do the Wolfsies do? Well, we all love to read. My wife reads lots of fiction; I read tons of nonfiction; even my son is an avid reader. Okay, we are readers. But this doesn't have much impact in a conversation.

"So Chuck, what did you and Sylvia do over Labor Day?"

"Oh, we took our 11 kids sky diving. What did you do, Dick?"

"Some pretty exciting stuff. We sat around sea level and read."

Many of you are probably feeling sorry for Mary Ellen and me. You think that our lives seem pretty dull, lacking any real avocations. Not so. We saw 45 movies last year, read 78 books, ate out 67 times and went to the American Cabaret Theatre twice. But if it weren't for the *New York Times* crossword puzzle, I could honestly say that my free time is totally devoid of anything that could remotely be held responsible for my breaking a sweat.

I know my wife and I should develop some exciting hobbies, but I'm over 50 now, and I'm actually thinking of cutting back to about 38 movies a year. My wife, however, is convinced we need more excitement.

"Let's make a resolution, Dick, that we will try to do at least one life-threatening activity every year. Don't you think that will keep us young?"

"No, but it might keep us from getting any older."

"How about Xtreme Skateboarding lessons?"

"What a great idea! You know that bashful little right knee of mine has been hiding in its socket for five decades. This might be just the ticket to coax it out.

"How about parasailing?"

"Great! That would kick in my fear of both heights and depths."

"Snowboarding, then."

"Sorry."

"You have said no to every idea I've had."

"I might consider that spelunking thing, but only after."

"After what?"

"After I look it up in the dictionary."

Power Struggle

Recent events have encouraged me to seek a change in the balance of power in my house. For the most part when there is any disagreement in the Wolfsie household, my wife and my son pretty much agree with each other. This voting bloc has been a source of irritation.

"Dick, let's go out for pizza."

"I don't know, Mary Ellen, I think Chinese sounds good."

"Dad, I vote for pizza."

So that pretty much seals my fate. I'm a big advocate of the democratic process, especially in the Senate and House. It's my own house that I'm beginning to question. Maybe it's just my imagination, but if my wife had said, "Hey, let's try that new spinach soufflé restaurant," my son would have still given her the deciding vote. I am not suggesting that my wife is exercising any undue influence, but I am a bit suspicious of Brett's one-sided allegiance.

"Brett, I've given this some thought and I want you to become an independent."

"What does that mean, Dad?"

"I want you to be non-partisan."

"Which means…?"

"Well, stop acting like an ideologue."

"Dad, you did a better job explaining sex to me."

"Brett, what I'm trying to say is that there are only three of us in the family. When Mom and I have a minor disagreement, you always side with Mom. Your one-sided view, especially on domestic issues, has given Mom an unfair advantage. I think we need to come to some kind of understanding."

"Dad, are you trying to bribe me?"

"Of course not. Let's just say I'm trying to lobby you."

"Dad, I'm not sure a fourteen-year-old like me can appreciate that distinction."

"I'm not sure a United States congressman can appreciate that distinction."

Brett's status as an only child has heightened his influence and there have been times when I thought that having more children would have lessened the chances of a minor wielding so much power. I don't think that kind of authority should be vested in one child who prefers playing video games to reading the United States Constitution. Nevertheless, I decided to negotiate.

"Brett, on what specific issues can we come to some understanding?"

"Well, Dad, I don't like your stance on school choice."

"School choice? What's wrong with my position

on school choice?"

"You want me to go to school every day. And I have no choice. Right?"

"Yes, that's correct."

"I rest my case."

"Very funny. What else?"

"Well, Dad, your view of appropriations."

"Appropriations? What on earth are you talking about?"

"You give me only five bucks a week for an allowance, right?"

"Yes."

"I don't think that's appropriate."

"Look, Brett what's your biggest gripe about my political views?"

"Dad, I listen to you on TV and the radio and you sound very liberal, but the truth is that while you broadcast on the left, you discipline on the right."

"You know, Brett, I think this discussion has gone far enough. Now you can either clean your room or mow the lawn. It's up to you."

"What does this have to do with your political views?"

"Let's just say I'm pro choice."

Too Timing Guy

When is it an appropriate time to ask friends what they are doing New Year's Eve? This seems like an odd question to come from a mature man, but it's coming from me, so there's nothing odd about it.

As a humorist, you would think that timing would be my forte. Humor depends on the perfect rhythm of words as they are strung together in sentences that can't be too long or too short.

Yes, timing is everything. Which is why I'm wondering if that should have been the opening line of this piece. Do you think I waited too long to say "timing is everything"?

See how insecure I am about this?

When I was a teenager I used to obsess over what day of the week to ask a girl out. If I asked too early in the week, like on Monday night, I always felt that she'd say no, hoping to get a better deal from a better looking guy on Wednesday night. Of course, if I asked too late, like Thursday night, she already had a better deal from a better looking guy so I was out of luck. Those last two sentences just kind of sum up my entire adolescence.

But now that I'm 50ish, (and it's the "ish" that's killing me), I still seem a little unsure about when to approach people for a commitment like New Year's Eve. When our son was just a toddler, I suffered the same anxiety in calling a babysitter, still not sure of the right way to time the communication. Finding a babysitter for New Year's Eve requires special skills and I'm not sure I ever mastered them.

"Hello, Jennifer, this is Mr. Wolfsie across the street. You know, the big 2000 New Year's Eve is coming up soon and I wondered if you were available to babysit. I hope I'm not calling too early."

"Well, I'd have to ask my mother, Mr. Wolfsie. You know I'm only eight years old."

"I know, but remember that it's only 1995."

Of course, now that I'm married, my son is grown and I'm a self-confident man with a successful career, you'd think I'd have this thing figured out. I'm still a little unsure with my own wife...

"Well, Mary Ellen, what should we do New Year's Eve?"

"Heavens, Dick, it's still three weeks away. What's the rush?"

"I've never gotten over my insecurity about this. I guess that there's still a part of me that will always be afraid some better looking guy will call you?"

"How flattering. But don't worry. We're married. I have to go with you."

"You sure know how to say the right thing."

Then there's the question of when to ask friends to go out on New Year's Eve. I used to think that Thanksgiving was a good time to ask, but when I would mention New Year's Eve plans in November, people would say things like: Geez, Dick, let me get through Thanksgiving. I can't possibly think about New Year's.

Then I would wait until after Thanksgiving and people would say: Geez, Dick, I have enough trouble thinking about Christmas. So last year, I waited until after Christmas to call our friends.

"Hi, Pat. I was wondering if you and Gerry wanted to get together New Year's Eve."

"You mean, like this year?"

"Yes, this year."

"Gee, Dick, sorry, but we've had plans with Tom and Irene for almost a month. You need to time this a little better."

"So, I guess this other couple must have been better timers."

"Yes, and better looking, too."

Life Changing Experience

I got a letter in the mail the other day that was pretty special and I'd like to share it with you.

Dear Dick,

Thank you so very much for your sensitivity, generosity and kindness. You will never know what a difference you made in my life.

Jerry

I just had one question. Who's Jerry?

Mary Ellen thought I was making this up.

"How can you not know who Jerry is? You changed his life."

"I know, I know, but the name doesn't ring a bell."

"Fine, but doesn't the changing his life part ring a bell?"

This was very frustrating for me because I'm not really that wonderful a guy and I usually don't do a great deal of life changing. In fact, I'd say I change someone's life only about once every six or eight years, so you'd think I'd remember a guy named

Jerry. Nope. Not a clue.

I went back through my appointment book to see if I had made any appointments that had life-altering possibilities.

It was actually kind of depressing because I saw no potential in the last six months for any such accomplishment. In fact, I didn't have much evidence in my appointment calendar for any displays of sensitivity or generosity. Truth is, if I had gotten a letter from someone saying:

Dear Dick:
You insensitive, ungenerous lout. You are not
a very kind person. Thanks for messing up my
life.

...well, a letter like that I could understand. That could have been from anybody.

But this one? Jerry? Jerry?? Wait a second, maybe it wasn't Jerry at all. Maybe it was his wife, or his son, or his daughter whose life I changed and that's why I couldn't place the name. Of course! And all this time I had been berating myself for not remembering Jerry's wife. I'm glad that's over. Now it won't bother me.

God help me. Who is Jerry?

Wait, I had an idea. I went to my computer and typed in "Jerry." Now we were getting somewhere. There were two million Websites with the name Jerry—the first 200 had something to do with gourmet ice cream, the next 300 were fan clubs for *Leave It to Beaver* and 250 more were for Jerry Springer.

I don't like Ben and Jerry's Ice Cream. When I eat it, my head freezes up and I get a terrible headache, but I don't think that's the kind of sensitivity Jerry meant.

I started to wonder if I had ever affected Jerry Mathers' life. I interviewed him once on my TV show and told him how much I loved the show where he got caught in the gigantic coffee cup on the billboard. I also told him that Eddie Haskell was a jerk and a slime, so I don't think I earned the sensitivity label. Nah. Not Jerry Mathers.

And Jerry Springer? Wow, I've met him also. But I don't think he even knows the words "kind" and "sensitive."

I tried to narrow the search on the computer: Jerry/Dick/Generous/Sensitive. Nothing. Not one example came up. Well, there was my answer. Jerry may have thought I changed his life, but I didn't. That's why I couldn't remember. It was some random act of kindness that I bestowed on someone— someone whose name I never got.

I started feeling better about myself. I had helped someone and asked for nothing in return. Not even the person's name. I am a kind and generous guy. I have changed a life and I had no motive other than the knowledge that I made a difference. I was content.

Please, God, who is Jerry?

Party Time

For most of you, the Millennium New Year's Eve is already a distant memory. Some of you, of course, can't remember it at all and you should be ashamed of yourselves.

Some of you stayed home and said something really obnoxious to friends: "Oh, we never go out New Year's Eve. New Year's Eve is amateur night." Of course, there were those of you who did go out for the second year in a row and got totally wasted with the excuse that this was the "real" beginning of the new millennium. You can get away with this twice every thousand years, but don't try it next December 31. Even people with no formal education and in the middle of their fourth vodka gimlet know that the official beginning of the new millennium is not 2003.

The other night my wife and I sat down and tried to remember what we did every New Year's Eve since we were married in 1980. We went backwards from last year and were doing pretty well until we hit the 80s.

"What did we do in '89, Dick? I can't remember."

"Wasn't that the year we took your sister to dinner?"

"I don't have a sister. I thought that was your sister."

"How about '88, Dick? Wasn't that the year we just got a bottle of Champagne and walked hand-in-hand in the park while the snow fell gently on our faces?"

"That doesn't sound remotely familiar."

"Sorry, Dick, that wasn't you in '88, that was Rick in '78."

"Okay, Mary Ellen. I remember '87. That was the year we rented a video, bought some popcorn, curled up on the couch and waited for the New Year to ring in."

"As I recall, you fell asleep at 9:30."

"I don't know why they can't do that falling ball thing around 8:45."

The more Mary Ellen and I talked, the more obvious it became that we have never been to a real New Year's Eve party. Don't misunderstand, it's not that we have never been invited to a New Year's Eve party, it's just that, well actually, come to think of it, we never have been invited to a New Year's Eve party. This was an eye opening revelation that Mary Ellen felt required some analysis.

"We have a very bad New Year's Eve record, Dick."

"I'd be proud of that. My brother's record on New Year's Eve cost him his license."

"You know what I mean. We have never been

invited anywhere. We often stay home. Sometimes we go out with close friends and have dinner, but we never get invited to go to a really big bash. I think one of us is the problem."

"Really?"

"Yes, I think one of us tends to have just a little too much to drink and then talk endlessly about himself and how television has changed over the years and why Ralph Nader should be president and how radio talk show hosts are too conservative. And then there's this endless harangue about how smart beagles are."

"I don't do any of that!"

"Well, aren't we insecure? I didn't say it was you."

Her premise was hard to argue with. I'm sure that without me, Mary Ellen would be invited to all the right places. I mean, she's attractive, well-mannered, and intelligent. Once at a company Christmas party, I observed her actually listening to someone who was talking to her. Wow! That's a hard act to follow.

"Dick, I think the answer to this problem is to have our own party next year."

"Great idea, Mary Ellen, but who would we invite? I mean, no one has ever invited us to their party and I'm sure not going to invite a bunch of ungrateful, insensitive people who didn't have the courtesy to include us in their celebrations."

"Boy, that Christmas spirit of yours just zings right over into the New Year."

"Before we get too depressed, consider this for

next year: A boardwalk, expensive hotel, spending money. Hours of non-stop fun. Sound like romance?"

"Knowing you, it sounds like Monopoly."

Forgotten Times

As if things weren't bad enough, what with the economy on the decline and the president on *West Wing* facing impeachment (I don't think I can go through this again), now I think I've been deprived of my favorite excuse: "Sorry, I forgot."

I don't mean just me. Just about everybody has lost this time-honored and effective explanation for being late or totally spacing out an important appointment. But I think I'm feeling the loss more than most.

It wasn't too many years ago that I could forget something and dismiss the entire incident by simply saying: "Geez, I'm sorry, was that your 75th anniversary? Oh well, I'll remember the next big one." Or I could say, "Sylvia, I know you said you needed a lift home from orthopedic surgery; it just slipped my mind."

This cavalier dismissal of responsibility just doesn't fly anymore. Technology has gotten so sophisticated that we have no excuse for not remembering. Instead, we depend on Palm Pilots, wristwatch alarms, computer calendars, and cell phones to prod us into remembering every important date. I see people every day poking at their Pilots just hoping that an appointment they have forgotten will pop up, thus justifying three months' grocery budget blown on an Etch-a-Sketch with e-mail.

"Hey, look at this, Harry. My Palm Pilot has just reminded me that my wife is having quintuplets at 4 p.m. today. Boy, would I be in the doghouse if I had forgotten that.

I think this is a very bad trend. For the past 20 years, I have depended on the act of forgetting to increase my work output. Let me explain. If I can't use "I forgot" as an excuse, I'm going to have to cut back on the number of commitments I make.

Why, just last week I promised my wife that on Saturday I'd fix the garage door. I also told my son I'd play golf with him, and I accepted a small stipend to speak to the Lions Club. I also asked my friend Norm to play tennis with me. You'd have to be a total idiot to think you could squeeze all that into eight hours. But I figured I'd legitimately forget a few of those obligations, thus freeing up some time. This concept has always worked for me in the past.

Years ago, my forgetfulness had a certain charm. It was not just an indicator of advancing age, it reflected a certain eccentricity. "Isn't he cute," I'd hear women whisper "and he can't remember anything he's supposed to do. He must be very bright."

Now that the word is out that I don't have a Palm Pilot or a talking wristwatch or an alarm clock with an attitude, people are skeptical about my commitments.

"So, Dick, can I absolutely, positively depend on you to be at the kindergarten read-in by noon?"

"How could I forget something as important as that?"

"May I ask what M.O.R. you'll be using?"

"Excuse me?"

"M.O.R. That stands for METHOD OF REMEMBRANCE. What state-of-the-art technology will you use to assist yourself in not blowing this appointment? If desired, we can assist you by interfacing with your cell phone, sending a signal to your Palm Pilot or making a subspace connection with your digital watch."

"Can you just call and remind me to read the crumpled wad of paper in my jeans pocket?"

I'm doing my best lately to remember all my obligations. I do use some of the more traditional M.O.R.s like sticky notes, finger strings, word associations and mnemonic devices. My wife's birthday is coming up, for example, and I don't want to forget it. I'm thinking about giving her a very special gift. But I want it to be a big surprise. I haven't even told my cell phone.

Party Politics

Here are a few things I had for dinner last night: eleven mini egg rolls, six tiny quiches and 12 cute little meatballs. I didn't know who to thank, Mary Ellen or Sam's Club.

My wife, you see, defrosted the basement freezer.

"Why am I having this for dinner, Mary Ellen?"

"It's left over from our big party last year."

"So why don't we use it for this year's party?"

"Heavens no. It was in the freezer an entire year. Who knows if it's still good."

I would have laughed at that remark, but it's hard to show amusement when you have six year-old cocktail franks in your mouth.

Truth is, Mary Ellen doesn't defrost very often, but when it's time, it requires a family meeting.

"Mary Ellen, it's that time again."

"Oh, Dick, is it four years already?"

"Yes, it's time to make the big decision: Defrost the freezer in the basement, or move."

"Oh dear, defrost or move, move or defrost. What do we usually do?"

"Well, Mary Ellen, we've lived in Indy for 20 years and have moved five times. Do the math."

Next thing I know, there's Mary Ellen, ice pick in hand, plunging her clenched fist into the encrusted ice—and in the process creating for me that night my most frightening nightmare in 20 years. I won't give you the details, but ever since that little dream, anything Mary Ellen wants, Mary Ellen gets.

But the point of all this, blunt as it may be, is to show how the Wolfsie house is affected by the prospect of entertaining. As a kid, I was always intrigued by that word, "entertaining," because I had visions of my mother and father wearing caps and bells and frolicking in front of the guests as they inhaled the spinach dip.

Truth is, my wife spends a great deal of time preparing for a party. She wants everything to be absolutely first class. The good news for me is that because of her obsession with perfection, I am assigned absolutely no responsibilities. As a result, I yearn for some way to put my personal stamp on the festivities.

I have been known to repaint the tree house, clean out the gutters, Turtle Wax the Taurus—anything to earn a little credit for a dynamite bash. One year I completely cleaned out the garage, shellacked the cement floor and repainted the walls. My wife was very happy to see me occupied so as not to upset her perfectly crafted preparation plans (but she was clearly opposed to my idea of serving the shrimp appetizers on the hood of the car). Then there was this year...

"Dick, why are you cleaning the crawl space?"

"Mary Ellen, I'm surprised at you. A clean house is a basic prerequisite to a successful party."

"Well, you're probably right. A couple of trips to the punch bowl and before you know it everyone will want to go downstairs and roll around in spider webs and mouse droppings. Hey, a party is a party."

Another big issue when we give a party is what to do about the floor. I'm a big advocate of shampooing the beige carpet the day after 40 people have trampled red wine, salsa, and avocado dip into it, but my wife always lobbies for shampooing before the party. Only a total boob in the art of debate could possibly lose this particular argument.

"Well, Dick, you've made some good points. So we'll compromise. You can shampoo the carpets before AND after the party. There's just no debating a guy as sharp as you."

Now most husbands, when they are outsmarted like this, just don't know where to put themselves. I do: I have the cleanest crawl space in the neighborhood.

Lost Causes

I spent the better part of two hours the other day looking for my glasses. You won't believe where I found them. No, not on top of my head. They were in my briefcase. What's that? Oh, you would believe that? Well, this is a problem because this whole thing is based on the premise that finding these glasses in my briefcase was very bizarre.

Let me try a different approach. When you lose something, do you ever go back and look in the same place several times? When I can't find my wallet, I check the back pocket of my pants about six or eight times. This is kind of silly. Admit it—you do it, too.

But back to my glasses. I couldn't find my glasses so I looked in my briefcase. They weren't there. So I looked there about eight times. The ninth time I looked, there they were. When things like this happen, I look to my wife for guidance. She has a way of putting some of my shortcomings in perspective.

"It's real simple, Dick. You don't look very good. You're just not good looking."

"You need to rephrase that, Dear. My ego is already bruised."

"Maybe my English is a little rusty. Let's say you don't look well."

"So, I need a doctor?"

"You're twisting my words. You're a loser. Just accept it."

"I should have quit when I needed a doctor."

"First of all, you're not logical. The other day you couldn't find the pants to your tuxedo. What did you do?"

"I went back to the church where we attended a wedding and looked under the pews."

"I rest my case. Looking for something also requires patience. The other day you reached for your wallet in your back right pocket. It wasn't there. What was the first thing you did?"

"I stopped all 35 credit cards. Do you think I over-reacted?"

"And where was your wallet?"

"It was in my left back pocket. But I didn't want to lose any valuable time."

Of course, no one likes to lose things. We don't like to lose a war, lose a game, lose our patience, lose a friend or lose a bet. You can also lose your way or lose your timing. I often lose my sense of direction. Many times in my career I have lost out. We've all lost a true love. In each of these phrases, the word "lose" or "lost" has a slightly different meaning. This last paragraph has nothing to do with my glasses, but I'm an old English teacher and

I couldn't pass up the opportunity.

Back to my glasses. I finally found them in my briefcase where, as I stated earlier, I had looked several times. I have developed three logical explanations for my failure to find them the first try. Guys, especially, feel free to use as many of these as you want:

1. My wife, scheming to drive me to suicide and collect the insurance, removed the glasses from my briefcase and then replaced them after I looked there eight times.

2. My son, scheming to drive me to suicide to get more time playing Nintendo, removed the glasses from my briefcase and then replaced them after I looked there eight times.

3. Barney, scheming to drive me to suicide so he could begin a career on his own, removed the glasses from my briefcase and then replaced them after I looked there eight times.

Those are my explanations and I'm sticking to them. I know what you're thinking. I seem a bit obsessed by this whole incident. You're afraid I'm on the edge.

Gee, I hope I'm not losing it.

Thanks for the Memories

Whenever baby boomers or senior citizens forget something, they think that they are losing their memories because they are getting older. Nothing could be farther from the truth.

That's why most people do not brag about their memories. It puts them under too much pressure. You seldom hear someone say, "I never forget a name or a face." Instead, people often brag about their shortcomings in this area. "I am so terrible with names. I hope you'll forgive me Ted, I mean Sheila."

I started thinking about this the other day as I looked through some old videotapes. Here I am, for example, interviewing Ed Asner, a well-known actor on shows like *Mary Tyler Moore*. If you had asked me a month ago if I had ever met Ed Asner, I'd have said no. But there I was. True, it was 20 years ago, but I'm still very depressed about this. I mean, what good is a memorable experience, if you can't remember it?

You can quote me on that.

Here's something else that scares me. I can't remember a great deal of my childhood. I know you're starting to wonder if I drink, but I swear that's not it. I keep trying to get a picture of myself sitting at the kitchen table with my brother and sister, something I probably did 10,000 times, but I can't remember where I sat. I also have no recollection of where I did my homework. I don't remember how I actually got to school each day. This made me so nervous, I decided to call my mother in New York.

"Mom, it's Dick. I have a question for you."

"Who is this?"

I guess it runs in the family.

Thousands of studies have been done about memory, but few can explain this common scenario:

"Joe, it was the most frightened I've ever been in my life. The parachute just wouldn't open."

"My God, Tom, this is an incredible story. Then what happened?

"Hold on, Joe. I have something in my eye. That's better. Now what were we talking about?"

"I don't have a clue."

"Me either. So how's your golf game?"

Memory is also very selective. Several years ago I was stopped by a woman in a parking garage who recognized me...

"Hey—Dick Wolfsie! Bet you don't remember me."

"Sure, you're Terry Terman from Muncie. You were on my show six years ago with your husband Tom. You have quadruplets named Toni, Todd, Ty, and Taylor."

She was very impressed with me. I was very impressed with me. Then I went into the parking lot and I couldn't remember where I parked my car. After two hours, I called my wife.

"Mary Ellen, you're not going to believe this."

"Don't tell me. You can't find the car again. How can you be so forgetful?"

"Okay, smarty pants. You name the Terman quadruplets."

Of course, my wife remembers almost everything. Almost. Unlike me, she has a clear image of large land masses that we have visited, like Europe. She remembers the month and day of her birthday... not the year. My wife can tell you the name of every actress and actor in every old movie. She can't tell you how much money she got out of the ATM machine.

And finally, my wife remembers when I forget to open the door for her, but she forgets when I remember. I saved this sentence for last because I think you'll need to read it a few times. What I'm trying to say is that she remembers when I forget, but when I forget, then this is something that she usually...In other words, it's easy for her to remember something that's...What I mean is...

Oh, forget it.

Potpourri

A tribute to kids, Barney, my mother and Steve Allen. Plus, a hodgepodge of other essays that didn't fit into any category, but without them the book would have been too short.

Eating Arrangements

All of our New Year's resolutions last January involved our son, Brett. When we were first married, Mary Ellen and I resolved to exercise regularly, read better books, spend quality time together, and give more to charity. Not any more. I guess when you get on in years, you figure that you're beyond self-improvement, so it's time to start imposing your good wishes on innocent children.

One of my wife's New Year's resolutions was to get our son to eat different foods. Like any kid, he loves burgers and fries, and pizza. He also loves stuff in a can like Chef Boyardee ravioli, Beefaroni and spaghetti. Mary Ellen thinks anything in a can is bad for you. As a result, all my six-packs of Bud are in bottles. After 20 years of marriage, I'm not looking for an argument.

When I was a kid, my German-born grandmother was on a similar mission, but while my wife and I would be thrilled if Brett would venture into grilled chicken and baked potatoes, Mum Mum (that's what I called her) wanted me to cultivate a taste for German cheeses. Mum Mum ate this Liederkranz cheese every day to the dismay of everyone who lived in her apartment house. So bad was the smell, that Mum Mum often got calls from concerned neighbors fearing she had passed away and no one had found her. When Mum Mum died at 96, we buried both her and the remaining cheese.

But back to Brett. When I walked into the kitchen the other day, Mary Ellen was explaining to Brett her new reward system that we were going to use on our family cruise to Alaska.

"It's very simple, Brett. If you eat a food that you hate, but you eat it three nights in a row, you get a dollar. But if you try a new food and you love it, then you don't get paid, unless it's a food that is really good for you and you eat it for a month. Now if you continue to eat foods that are bad for you and they are old foods, you pay us a dollar, but if they are new bad food, there is no exchange of money."

"Boy, Mom, what two-hour period in your life did you take off to think of that?"

Actually, the idea of a monetary reward seemed pretty good until I walked into the kitchen the other night and witnessed Brett with a huge bowl of rocky road ice cream covered with sweet and sour cabbage.

"Are you okay, Brett? Your face is all contorted. Does it taste funny?"

"Just confused, Dad. Do I owe you money or do

you owe me money?"

For the next couple of weeks, the plan worked pretty well. Brett tried a number of different foods, but I wasn't happy with the system.

"No offense, Mary Ellen, but this idea of yours has cost us eighty-five bucks. Plus, he orders only expensive items now. Look, he's only thirteen. It wouldn't kill him to eat off the kids' menu until we emancipate him."

"You are so shortsighted. Brett says he now loves okra, anchovies, goat cheese, and squid.

"Oh boy, let the feast begin. By the way, did it ever dawn on you that both of us hate all four of those foods? And we never have them in the house. Where on earth did he try them?"

"Today, at school."

"How time flies. Was it Armenian Day again in the cafeteria?"

I shouldn't make too much fun of the system. This week, for example, has gotten much better, but I still think the plan has some flaws. At dinner last night at a fancy restaurant, I noticed Brett eating something new...

"Well, Dad, instead of chicken fingers and fries, I ordered the blackened swordfish, the steamed beets, and the spinach soufflé. For dessert I'm going to experiment with the crème brulee. How does that sound?"

"Nutritionally?"

"No, financially. I'm saving up for a case of Beefaroni."

Spreading the News

Can we talk about condiments? You know, mustard, ketchup, and mayonnaise. I'd include tartar sauce, but you don't see a great deal of tartar sauce nowadays. You probably have had a jar in your fridge for years. Open it up. If it smells funny, it's probably still okay. I'm actually surprised that I haven't written about condiments before. I have never even mentioned French's or Heinz or Gulden's in any of my stories. Considering my near obsession with condiments, this seems impossible.

Condiments must generally be a male thing. You would never hear a man say to his wife, "Golly, with all that ketchup on the burger, Sweetheart, you can't possibly appreciate the fine texture and flavor of the grain-fed beef." Women, on the other hand are more apt to say: "If you put ketchup on my Chicken Kiev, I will rip your ruby-red tongue right out of your mouth."

Of all the condiments, mustard still has my vote

for tastiest. I did some research on the Internet and discovered that there are about 100 different kinds of mustard, but basically, there is only one kind of ketchup. There are gourmet mustards—mustards you would gently brush on a $75.00 rack of lamb— but there is no gourmet ketchup that I am aware of. I would welcome a good gourmet ketchup. I think most Hoosiers would. Somebody is missing a golden opportunity here. I know you're still kicking yourself for not thinking of designer water first, so don't let this gourmet ketchup thing get away.

I don't want to brag, but I have improved just about every dinner my wife has ever prepared by carefully adding the appropriate condiment. What would her chicken marsala be like without my mayonnaise? Uneventful, that's what. How would her Beef Bourguignon taste without mustard? I shudder to think. And what about her Veal Oscar without ketchup? Lifeless. And I'm being generous. Okay, enough bragging. Here's some final advice.

1. You can leave mustard and ketchup on your dining room table overnight and still put it safely back in the fridge the next day. Don't do this with mayonnaise. There is an entire cemetery in Brooklyn, New York, filled with people who hid a pastrami sandwich from their spouse, putting it under the bed, but forgetting that Russian dressing is half mayonnaise.

2. When placing mustard on a sandwich, ALWAYS put the mustard in between the meats on the bread. Mayonnaise, however, needs to go on

the top of the meat. Ketchup can go either way. Never apply condiments directly to the bread. This information is the result of a grant by the United States Government to a national taste-testing institute. Finally, tax money well spent.

3. Turn upside down and shake all plastic bottles vigorously before squeezing mustard or ketchup on your sandwich. Nevertheless, the bottle will still make an embarrassing sound. If you want a laugh from your kids, just say, "excuse me" after it squirts. It's foolproof.

4. NEVER buy mayonnaise in a squeeze bottle. Mayonnaise belongs in a glass jar. Buying mayonnaise in a plastic squeeze bottle would be like buying whipped cream in a box. It's not normal. It's un-American. The manufacturers should be arrested. Where is the FBI when you really need them? Probably at the airport. Finally, I think that it is important that kids learn about ketchup, mayonnaise and mustard at home. I don't want the public school system passing out condiments in the cafeteria. I think it should be up to the parents.

Dog Talk

For several years now, my dog, Barney, has been yapping about wanting to write a newspaper column for me. I have resisted this, but at the last Channel 8 Christmas party, Barney was given an award for 10 years of service to the TV station. This has to be some kind of a milestone, not just for a dog, but for anyone who has the doggedness to stick with something for so long. Especially television. So, for this one time, the word processor is his. Go for it, Barney!

Thanks, Dick. First I want to say that Dick and I have done almost 3,000 TV shows together. That's 9000 segments, and about 20,000 guests. For ten years we have gotten up at 3:30 a.m. and we have never missed a show by oversleeping. We are both dog-tired.

Once we get to our remote location, the fun starts. We have to organize three segments, be sure all the guests know their parts, check that all the names are spelled correctly and that my cameraman, Carl, has some idea what Dick and I are going to do. All three of us work like dogs. Especially me.

On location, I usually have to do some kind of a segment that in some way humiliates me. I've been dressed as a woman, gotten pies in my face, been buried in a stone quarry, been covered with Jello, wrestled in the mud and worn funny hats. This is something that Channel 8 wants me to do. Sometimes I'd rather not. No one likes being treated like a dog. Again, especially me.

Wolfsie and I do try very hard to give you great TV because the other stations are always trying to beat us. The competition is very stiff, especially during ratings. Everyone's looking for the best stories and would do anything to crush the underdog. It's a dog-eat-dog world. Not very appetizing.

But my job is fun. The hardest part is convincing people to be on the show that early in the morning. Lots of times Wolfsie and I have to do some serious cajoling and persuading. When people say no at first, we hound them a little bit. (That's *my* job.)

The executives at Channel 8 have always been a little wary of us. You see, Wolfsie and I do live TV. We never know what is going to happen or what we are going to say. There's a chance we could say or do something that would be very embarrassing and even get Channel 8 in trouble. That makes the bosses uneasy. So they watch us like dogs.

Usually the show is pretty good, but occasionally it's really amazing. In fact, sometimes Dick comes home with an inflated view of himself. Every dog has his day, you know. Even humans.

Of course, sometimes the show is really bad. That's when we both get depressed. Then, Dick feels like dog meat. Sounds good to me.

There are great aspects of my job. I get to meet interesting people and go to new places. Dick and I have probably met more wonderful people in this town than anyone else in television. Hey, it's a dog's life.

One final note: Don't give Dick any credit for making me a star. Quite the contrary. Before he found me I was already doing just fine, working the streets with my act and eking out a living. When I joined WISH-TV, I made Dick a star. Talk about the tail wagging the dog!

Well, that's it. My column is over.

Doggone it.

Barney

Back to School

It had been 20 years since I had gone back to my old high school in New Rochelle, New York. There were lots of memories because I had been both a student and a teacher there.

I remembered how nervous I was entering those doors on my first day of high school in 1962. And even more nervous back in September of 1969, when at the age of 22, I was hired to teach high school seniors the subject of psychology—something I knew little about, having taken only one course in college.

I walked into the main office. Here was a place I had entered 200 times in the 70s as a teacher to get my paycheck handed to me, and about 200 times in the 60s as a student to get my head handed to me.

The main office was more modern, of course—a computer on every desk, a sea of fresh faces. But the connecting long, narrow room where teachers picked up their mail was exactly the same. I walked over to where my mailbox used to be, half convinced that my name would still be on it. (Don't they retire mailbox numbers for terrific teachers?) I even slid my hand through the narrow opening. Maybe an old memo with my name on it was still stuck in there, scrunched up in the back of the slot. I was somewhat miffed that a letter addressed to Troy Walters was in my box. MY box.

"May I help you?" asked a young secretary who apparently was a bit suspicious of what appeared to be mail tampering.

"Sorry, I used to be a teacher here."

As soon as the words came out of my mouth, I knew how lame they sounded. Imagine being picked up by the police in a bank robbery and saying, "It's okay, officer. I used to deposit money here."

"You need to sign in," she snipped, unimpressed that I was once one of New Rochelle High School's finest teachers in the 70s. It would have meant little to her: In the 70s, she was probably one of New Rochelle's crankiest toddlers.

I signed in, this time boasting to a hall security guard that I was once a teacher in this very building.

"Wait a second, weren't you a student here? I've been here 40 years. You were that goofy kid who was always in trouble and staying after school for being a wise guy in class. And then you were on TV here in New York for awhile and got fired after six months because the ratings were miserable."

"Wow, you sure have a good memory. Do you happen to remember that I was also here for ten years as one of New Rochelle High School's finest teachers in the 70s?"

"Sorry, I don't remember that. Are you sure that was you?"

He was kidding, I hope.

I walked backed to the main office and smack into Don Baughman. Don had been my baseball coach. He also taught me history when I was in the 12th grade. Then we worked together in the Social Studies department when I came back to teach.

"I remember coaching you in baseball, Wolfsie. Good fielder, but you couldn't hit a lick. We used to put you in the game in the 8th inning so you couldn't bat. And you sure were a cut-up in class. Say, what happened to that bomb of a TV show you did on Channel 7?"

"Say, Don, do you happen to remember that I taught here in the 70s? I was one of New Rochelle High School's finest teachers."

"No kidding? Which department?"

He was kidding, I hope.

I left the school a little depressed. Virtually every one of my former colleagues was retired, and a few had passed away. But I was looking forward to breakfast with a former student. Reuben is now a school principal out on Long Island.

"You know, Mr. Wolfsie, you were a great influence on me. You always encouraged me to push myself and excel. I went into education because of you."

He wasn't kidding, I hope.

Alarming Mother

I'd like to take this opportunity to wish my mother a Happy Mother's Day. She is 82 years old. Joan is still an excellent driver, dresses to the nines, swims every day, and hasn't been home for lunch in 30 years. After my father died 10 years ago, Mom started dating the guy who dumped her in 1942. She said he'd suffered without her long enough.

Joan has always been young at heart and she confided to me recently that she feels like a 17-year-old girl inside. This made me a little nervous. I don't think most fathers even want their 17-year-old daughters to feel like they're 17 inside, so you can imagine how I feel about my mother. Yes, 82 can be a difficult age for some women. In this case, it's been more difficult for me.

Oh, I don't mind my mother feeling younger, but I would have picked a different number, like 43 or 57. If I told my wife I felt like 17 again, she'd probably have me followed.

As I write this tribute, I should tell you that Joan and I have had a little falling out. She called the other day and asked whether I thought she needed to buy an expensive burglar alarm system. Her house, a small ranch in the suburbs of New York, is the very same home that I grew up in. It's very modest; not the kind of house you'd want to break into. As a kid, I spent a lot of time trying to break out of the house. My father wanted me to get better acquainted with the four walls of my room. In fact, if you look up the "History of Grounding Your Teenager" in the *World Book Encyclopedia*, you'll see my dad's picture. But back to Joan.

"Dick, do you think I should buy a burglar alarm?"

"Of course! Wouldn't that give you peace of mind?"

"Yes, but there really haven't been that many break-ins in our neighborhood. Maybe I'll wait."

"Mom, you're 82. What are you waiting for?

"I don't know, a crime wave or a prison break. I just don't want to jump into something that I might never need. I wouldn't want to spend all this money and then never have a break-in. I want to be sure I'll use it."

"Mom, you get guarantees that something will work, not that you'll use it."

"I got a guarantee at Forest Lawn."

"A cemetery plot is different. Mom, there is a certain deterrent power to an alarm system. It prevents criminals from breaking and entering. If they see you have a burglar alarm, they'll go to a different house."

"Which house? Would they take a friendly suggestion?"

"No, Mom, but it would stop them from even trying to break in."

"Well, that is a good thing. But I'd like to track that. I want to distinguish between the crook who is scared off by my $3000 burglar alarm system and the ungrateful little hoodlum who thinks my house isn't worth the time to rob. What, because the basement isn't finished and we have a one car garage, I should be passed over?"

"What's stopping you from getting an alarm system?"

"Too expensive. Maybe they have cheaper models. Maybe just for thugs with guns."

"Mom, no skimping here. You don't want to wake up and find a man in your house."

"If he were single and unarmed, I could spring for $1500."

Okay, I've exaggerated a bit here, but the essence of this column is basically accurate. Joan wants a burglar alarm but is too cheap to buy one. Maybe I'll get her one for her 83rd birthday. But I do hope she really needs one. I'd hate to unnecessarily alarm her.

Wolfsie on Speed

In New York, everything moves very quickly. You have to talk fast, eat fast, think fast. Walking fast is usually a good idea, also. But everything is relative. You can walk fast, but cars and muggers also move fast, so you're never really out of danger. If you stand on a street corner in New York for too long, someone will steal your kneecaps. I think that's an old Rodney Dangerfield joke, but I once sold him a joke and he never paid me. Now we're even.

I'm going to New York to visit my mother. Then my brother. Then my sister. I think you can see from my sentence structure that I'm not looking for a family reunion. I just want to visit with loved ones but I don't want the whole thing ruined by a big emphasis on togetherness. You see, any differences you have as family are exaggerated when you live in New York.

I had a college friend from Maui. His father and mother split when he was four. They were both alcoholics. His sister burned down their house and his older brother once broke his arm with a baseball bat. They all get together at Christmas and talk about the good old days. If you come from Hawaii and your family is dysfunctional, you'll never notice.

But let's talk more about New York. On the way home in the car, my mother will remind me how the traffic has been bad in New York for the last 80 years. We'll probably then stop somewhere that "was never any good" for dinner. My brother, who is a cab driver, will say things like "I can't believe this construction. They've been building this bridge for 40 years."

In Indiana, we talk about how cheap things used to be. "I remember when gas was a quarter," I heard an Indiana woman tell her teenage son. In New York, nothing was ever cheap. Even in 1950, I think gas was still about two bucks a gallon. By the way, Central Park was never safe. It's so unsafe now no one ever goes there any more; plus it's too crowded, anyway. Yogi Berra once said something like that but unlike Rodney, Yogi never stole anything from me—except the '56 World Series (I was a Dodgers fan). As you can see, New Yorkers hold grudges. And they lose them slowly. It's the only thing New Yorkers do slowly.

The implication of all this is clear. New York is the only place in America that rejects the concept of "The Good Ol' Days." In New York, life has always been pretty miserable, and it's slowly not getting any worse. Most people around the country wax nostalgic about the past, but can also puff up a bit about the progress their city has made. Not New Yorkers. If you live in New York, you are proud of the fact that you have managed to tough it out for 30 years. If you admit things have gotten better, you'd risk paling in the eyes of those who admire your spunk and spirit. And if you get teary-eyed about the past, it looks like you once had it easy.

I look forward to being in New York. We have about a week of neat things planned. It should take us about three days to get it all done.

Escaping Logic

The other night after my family had finished a delicious meal of barbecued pork chops, stuffing and green beans, my wife and I were surprised to see our son scarfing down a can of Chef Boyardee ravioli.

"Brett, what in heaven's name are you doing?"

"Having dessert, Dad."

"Dessert? Dessert is cake, or pie, a cookie, maybe fruit. Not Chef Boyardee ravioli."

"Dad, dessert is not what you eat; it's when you eat it. I finished my dinner; dessert comes next. You could look it up."

I didn't look it up. I wanted him to be right. It's the kind of creative thinking that is not taught in the schools. Certainly not in the cafeteria. I decided to pursue this a little further.

"Brett, if we follow your theory, the main course could be ice cream and cake."

"Dad, I think you've got it. Good job! Now you can have that beer buffet for dinner you always talk about, and not feel guilty."

The more I talk to my son, the more I wish I were 14 again and could use his logic. Just last week, I walked out the front door, with Brett right behind me. I turned and I noticed the door still wide open, flapping in the wind. I wasn't happy.

"BRETT!"

"Yes, Dad?"

"Why didn't you close the front door?"

"Why should I? It's not logical."

"I think I need help with this one."

"Dad, you're not using your noggin. When I leave my bike in the driveway, you tell me to put it away. Why? Because I was the one who rode it."

"Go ahead, I'm still lost."

"Think about it, Dad. Who opened the door? You did. Not me. Try to be more responsible."

"Yes, but you see...the difference is...it's not the same because...well, what I'm saying is...hold on a second while I close the door."

I'm a victim of this kind of logic with my wife as well. It's a typical Saturday night and we're getting ready to go out. We are expected somewhere at 6:00 p.m. and it's 5:45...

"Mary Ellen, you have to hurry. We are late."

"No we're not. We don't have to be there until 6."

"Okay, I know I'm being a bit obsessive, but aren't we 45 minutes from the restaurant?"

"Just relax. We'll be fine."

Twenty minutes later, we get in the car. It's now 6:05.

"Well, Dick, are you satisfied? Now we are late.

Next time maybe you won't talk to me so much while I am getting ready."

Both my wife and son seem to have perfected a certain kind of logic that defies understanding. Here's another one my wife pulls on me when she returns from a shopping spree:

"Hi, Dick. Wait until you see how frugal I was today. All this stuff was on sale. I saved over $300.00."

"But you spent $1200.00. I guess I'm not feeling real lucky."

"You certainly are lucky. I could have saved $600.00."

She was right. That actually made sense. The next time she went shopping, I gave her a big hug at the door.

"Have a great day shopping, Dear. Try not to save too much money!"

"Why?"

"I don't think we can afford it."

Food Fright

USA Today reported last week on the ten most dangerous foods you can eat while driving. Accidents that occur while munching on these delicacies are called food-related wrecks. Just when you finally realize that holding a cell phone in your ear while reading a newspaper and making a U-turn is dangerous, now it appears that eating a taco can be just as deadly.

Fasten your seat belts—loosely—and listen to this: A group of scientists did extensive research into food-related accidents by getting in their SUVs and driving around hairpin turns while trying to eat Kentucky Fried Chicken. Apparently, it isn't the 90 grams of fat that kills you, or smacking into a pylon, it's parallel parking while licking your fingers.

The research lasted two years. Fortunately, there were no traffic deaths, but the 25 researchers gained 600 pounds and ruined four leather seat covers and 60 pairs of polyester pants.

The **Number 1** most dangerous food, by the way, was coffee. Piping hot coffee in the lap proved to be a distraction to almost everyone who had any kind of personal life when they got home. Most people kept their hands on the wheel when the coffee spilled, but cracked their heads wide open when they hit the roof and yelled something that sounded like Curly of the Three Stooges.

Hot soup was next. I don't know about you, but there's nothing better than a hot cup of cream of broccoli soup while driving to work in the morning. I manage it pretty well, but my wife insists on using a spoon. I think that's even more dangerous. In several cases, it wasn't spilling the soup that caused the distraction, but sprinkling on the croutons.

Number 3 was tacos. According to the research, tacos crumble easily and people try to catch the falling pieces, leaving no hands on the wheel. The police in California are really cracking down on this and they now have a Taco Breathalyzer Test. Fail it and they put you in a Tijuana slammer with an annoying little Chihuahua named Teddy.

Number 4 was called "chili-covered food." This causes accidents because women immediately try to blot the stain, while men bend over and try to lick the chili off their pants.

As I mentioned earlier, fried chicken was studied, and it made the list at **Number 7**. But here's the good news: grilled chicken, chicken piccata, chicken Florentine, chicken francaise—none of those made the list. Enjoy.

Number 8 was jelly doughnuts. I'm sorry, if you can't eat a Krispee Crème and drive safely on 465 you should get a home office. By the way, jelly doughnuts were not quite as dangerous as creme-filled. Good news if you are fighting both traffic and high cholesterol.

Number 9 was soft drinks. Apparently, accidents are caused by people looking down so they can get the cup into the holder. Dr. Pepper was more dangerous than Coke, but Mountain Dew was the most dangerous soft drink of all. Like you didn't know that.

The least dangerous food of the Top 10 was chocolate, but it still rated a potential threat. The researchers considered a Mounds candy bar the equivalent in danger to a high-speed blow-out. Sometimes it takes a Ph.D. to take the fun out of candy.

This is serious business. If you want to pig out in your car after barreling through a Wendy's or McDonald's drive-thru, consider climbing in the backseat to chow down. Then get a friend to drive.

Don't think of yourself as a glutton, think of yourself as a designated eater.

Goodbye, Mr. Allen

Steve Allen is gone. This is especially difficult for me to accept because Steve Allen is my hero. That's not a word you should throw around. There have been other people in sports and entertainment whom I have loved and admired. I loved Jack Benny. But he wasn't my hero. I adored Buster Keaton. He wasn't my hero, either. Duke Snider was a center fielder for the Brooklyn Dodgers. In the 1950s, he hit more home runs than anyone in baseball. And Sam Snead. I can tell you every major record he holds. But Sam and Duke were not my heroes.

When I watched Steve Allen on TV in the '50s, I remember being jealous. I spent many afternoons sitting in the hallway outside Mrs. Houseman's third grade classroom. I was being punished for "acting silly." I never thought of it as acting. Silliness is not something you do; it is something you are. I are it. And so was Steve Allen. I like sharing something with Steve Allen.

But Steve took silliness to new heights (or depths, if that's your preferred direction). And he did it before Paar, Carson, Letterman and Leno. His silliness was not a line on a cue card or script. It came from his very soul.

You have read about all of his incredible accomplishments: his books, TV shows, his music, even his movies. The pundits want you to know what an incredible intellect he was, what a Renaissance man. All of this is true. But what of silly?

So silly, he smeared his body with dog food and unleashed a pack of assorted dogs. So silly, he strapped a kite to his back and ran into a huge fan. So silly, he read letters from irate newspaper readers and went into a frenzy himself. So silly, that he put a live camera on the corner of Hollywood and Vine and commented on the people who walked by. So silly that he laughed at himself for laughing. Now that's silly.

All silly stuff. No affectation. No need to remind the audience that he was brilliant, that he composed music, that he could speak six languages, that he had written several books. Steve Allen was silly. And he was proud of it. That made him my hero.

I've met with Steve Allen four times. The first time was in New York when I hosted *Good Morning, New York*. During our interview, we were talking about the great comic actor, Stan Laurel. "You don't meet people of that ilk anymore," said Mr. Allen. "You could join the ilks club," I said. It was a Steve Allen kind of joke. And we both knew it. He laughed. No one laughed like Steve Allen. I didn't have to die. I was already in heaven.

Years later, I interviewed Steve Allen at the opening of MGM Theme Park in Disney World. At the time, *US Magazine* had come out with the 50 most influential people in the history of TV. Steve Allen wasn't on the list. Incensed, I did a takeoff of his old news reporter bit, slapping the magazine onto the desk in outrage. Mr. Allen laughed again. Can you go to heaven twice?

Three weeks later I got a personal note from Steve Allen. "I watched the tape of our interview. Very funny stuff," he wrote. "You did a good job." That letter hangs on my wall. I try not to read it more than ten times a day.

Two years ago, I interviewed Steve Allen when he was in Indy to give a lecture. Overall, I spent about an hour with my hero talking about our favorite subject: humor. After a somewhat intellectual discussion, I wanted him to know how much I had enjoyed watching him over the years, how much he had made me laugh. A little afraid I might insult him, I boldly went ahead...

"Mr. Allen," I said, "I have to tell you how silly I've always thought you were."

"Thank you," he said. "Thank you very much."

I'm sitting here alone at the computer right now. And I'm starting to cry. Silly, isn't it?

Strange Occurrences

A famous humorist once said that writing humor is easy. "When something funny occurs to you, you just write it down." The author went on to say: "The writing is easy; it's the occurring that's the hard part."

So there it was. I needed something to stimulate my occurring. In the past, I have depended on my wife to aggravate me, or my son to frustrate me, in order to stimulate my funny bone. But now I realized that I had been using them as a crutch. What I simply needed to do was to sharpen my occurring skills. This had, quite frankly, never occurred to me.

I figure that this is exactly what Dave Barry and Art Buchwald do. They walk around the house occurring. When they near a deadline they go to the office to occur, or to the supermarket. Professional humorists are great at occurring. Like Andy Rooney...

"Andy, Sweetheart, why are you separating the

peanuts from the walnuts in that can? It's three in the morning."

"Go back to bed, Dear. Can't you see I'm occurring?"

"You've been occurring for 50 years. Can't you just snore at night like normal men?"

Of course, I'm no Andy Rooney, so I needed to do my occurring on a much grander scale. I decided to walk around the house and see if any of the rooms in my house would stimulate an occurrence.

I decided to start occurring in the basement. I really shouldn't call it a basement. When we moved into the house, it was a basement, but we spent $15,000 to "finish" it. Actually, we finished 75% of the basement and left 25% for storage. It then occurred to me that the 75% that we finished was being used the exact same way as the 25% for storage. And then it occurred to me that I blew fifteen grand. I decided to go upstairs. Two occurrences were more than I could handle.

The laundry room seemed a good place to occur. As I entered the laundry room, it occurred to me that the kitty litter needed changing. But then it occurred to me that I really don't like cats. It's my wife who loves the cats. But it's my job to change the litter. It never occurred to me before how unfair this is. You can learn a lot about your marriage when you start occurring.

The attic seemed a good place to occur. Attics are always full of interesting artifacts that bring back memories. I could rummage around the attic, try on some old clothes, look at scrapbooks, and read through old letters. Something funny would certainly occur to me there. This seemed like the perfect plan. Then it occurred to me: We don't have an attic.

My wife suggested I go in the garage for an occurrence.

"Dick, don't you see what a disgusting mess it is, filled with old empty paint cans, floor mats, rusty tools, decayed fertilizer, animal droppings and rotting automobile tires? Doesn't it make you realize how desperately you need to clean it up?"

"Sorry, it never occurred to me."

I was getting desperate. My plan had failed. I was doing a heck of a lot of occurring, but it was all essentially humorless. But there was one place I had not yet occurred, a place just ripe for a funny occurrence: the kitchen. I raced into the room and swung open the refrigerator door. Suddenly, dozens of funny things started occurring to me. It occurred to me how many food items had passed their expiration date; it occurred to me how many tasteless non-fat foods were in our fridge; it occurred to me how many empty containers were on the shelves. I was in heaven. I told my wife all my hysterical occurrences.

"That's just great, Dick. But Dave Barry, Art Buchwald and Andy Rooney have already written about every one of those topics. Is that what you call occurring?

"Of course not. I call it reoccurring!"

No Laughing Matter

Editor's note: Written the week of 9/11/01

You probably need a good laugh. Things look pretty grim in the world. Yes, you need a laugh. And you deserve one. I just can't help you out. It was kind of strange in my basement last week. I sat in front of the computer trying to think of something funny to write. That's my job. Just to the right of me was my TV. I heard Peter Jennings, Tom Brokaw, Dan Rather, Wolf Blitzer and Tony Snow all reporting the horrible events of the week.

There was a part of me that knew I needed to ignore them and do my job. I had to write something funny. I guess I would have expected no less of others. I had a dental appointment. I wouldn't have wanted the hygienist to tell me that she was too depressed to clean my teeth. That's her job. She needed to get on with her life.

That was easy to say. I didn't believe a word of it. I even resented people giving me a friendly good morning the day after those horrific events. What were they so cheery about? Maybe they hadn't spent the last 35 hours in front of the TV watching those violent images of death and destruction. I did. I'm not sure why. I couldn't tear myself away.

I know my obsession with the news coverage went deeper than rubbernecking on a highway after an accident. It was a futile attempt to understand what had happened and why. That's giving Peter Jennings a lot of responsibility. Instead, I sat at my computer trying to be funny. It didn't happen.

All the experts will tell you that humor comes out of human tragedy, that all the great comics of our time came from a troubled childhood. Most jokes, they say, are a reflection of our own unhappiness and insecurity. I felt both those emotions. If that's true, why couldn't I think of anything funny? Because some events are so oppressively sad and tragic that they poison that bottomless well of potential comic material.

Jay Leno and David Letterman had a problem. Their job is to make fun of the events of the day. That worked for Bill Clinton's peccadilloes and George Bush's verbal goofs. But even sex and syntax didn't seem very funny last week.

That's why late night hosts did not do monologues, why baseball and football games were cancelled. Was this just for security reasons? Was it out of respect for those who perished? Yes to both, but I think for many people there was a need to be amusement-free for just a while. Maybe it was our own small way to share in the misery. I didn't want to have any fun this past week. I was pretty successful.

But here's what's important: We won't feel that way forever. Even the people most closely touched by this inexplicable human tragedy will laugh again. Not about these events, but in memory of the people they loved and with whom they shared special moments.

They probably won't laugh today. Or tomorrow. But someday.

And soon, I will think of something funny to write about my wife, my son, my dog and my job.

I just can't think of anything right now.

But someday.

Mark of Humor

In response to a nosey neighbor who once questioned Mark Twain as to why there were so many books piled high on his living room floor, Twain remarked: "It's hard to borrow shelves."

When I hear lines like that I am torn between wanting to believe that this was truly an ad lib or that Twain created the scenario and the retort while sitting in his armchair or behind his typewriter.

Both accomplishments would be equally admirable because the remark is a classic example of how the listener is amused in direct proportion to the amount of information he needs to fill in to understand the joke. Here, in a microsecond, the listener must synthesize several elements: that the books are borrowed, that Twain has no shelves, that shelves can't be borrowed, that Twain would borrow them if he could, etc, etc. This is coupled with the absurdity of the notion along with the basic logic of Twain's premise.

As you can see, the listener of a joke has a great deal of work to do.

Don't give up on me. Funny stuff is just around the bend.

A television reporter like myself takes great pleasure in all the clever things that he or she has said over the years. I'm no Mark Twain, although I've had my moments. But I'm in the holiday spirit already. So instead of bludgeoning you with my witticisms, I invite you to listen in on my favorites from my guests over the years...

Several years ago we had a Barney look-alike contest at Pet Supplies Plus. All contestants were given a slew of prizes just for entering, including free dog food and dog toys. The morning of the show, 42 beagles and their owners crowded into Pet Supplies Plus on Pendleton Pike. Forty-two beagles howling at the top of their lungs is great TV.

As the show opened, in walked a heavyset man with a chubby bulldog, huffing, puffing and drooling (the dog, not the man). Convinced that the owner had misunderstood the contest, I walked over to him during the commercial break.

"That's a bulldog," I whispered to him, as if he didn't know. His response was immediate.

"So? I'll lose."

About a year ago, I asked a very prominent local vet to do eye surgery on my morning show. The doctor agreed to actually replace the lens in an aging dog's eye, all on live TV. It was a great show. We watched the vet perform his delicate maneuvers on the anesthetized pooch. When the show ended, I couldn't help asking the surgeon what he would have done if the aging dog had "passed on" during anesthesia—a rare, but not unheard of, occurrence. Like my bulldog friend, his answer was classic:

"I'd have operated on a dead dog."

Several years ago I traveled to Anderson, Indiana, to a pet store that stocked a variety of exotic pets. One of the owner's personal friends was an 8-foot alligator that swam about in a huge enclosed area inside the store. When I arrived at the site, I was amused to see that the alligator was sporting a T-shirt that said "WISH-TV" on it. During the questioning of my guest, I asked:

"So, has anyone ever gotten in the tank with that alligator?"

"No, Dick. The alligator put the shirt on himself."

So there's proof that almost anyone can come up with a truly funny remark—given the right circumstances and a good straight line. Which leads me to believe that the great Mark Twain wrote his funniest stuff at the typewriter. That is truly the hardest thing to do. I know that all too well. Which is why this piece is filled with other people's funny lines.

Clown Suit

I'm not making this up. I read in the paper the other day that an organization called Clowns International is recommending to all their clown members that they take out pie insurance.

Apparently, this group is afraid that while no one has ever sued a clown for getting hit by a pie, it's just a matter of time before some loser who is allergic to rhubarb or cherries slaps some red-nose with a tort.

I know you're tempted to say, "Instead of a tort, why not just hit him back with a tart?" Hey, who's writing this humor book, anyway?

I am probably one of 280 million people in this country who has never sued a clown. Keep in mind, however, that on any given day some clown is suing a toilet seat manufacturer because he used his throne as a stepladder to change a light bulb and can't understand why he injured his groin. But it still doesn't seem right to sue a clown.

If a clown did get sued, what's the most a judge would throw at him? Community service? I'm sorry, community service for a clown is not punishment.

"Bozo, you have been found guilty of throwing a high cholesterol projectile. I sentence you to three months of not making people laugh."

"No, judge, anything but that. Please, I'll be a good person. No, I mean I'll be a bad person. I'm so confused."

Then there's... what I mean is,... sometimes clowns will... Wow! I have nothing left to say about clowns and lawsuits. I hate it when that happens. I sit down at the computer waiting to whip out about 700 words on a subject and then I find out that I really don't have that much to say. I'd like to stop right there, but that's not the way it is done. In the newspaper business, a columnist has to write a certain number of words. And even if you have nothing left to say, you need to keep writing. This happens with talking a lot. You really have nothing else to say on a topic, but you just keep chatting away. See? You, too, could be a humor columnist.

I feel the same way about news anchors. Just once I'd like Dan Rather to say at about 6:20 p.m., "There's really nothing else to report of any significance so I think I'll just go home and do something weird with my hair."

When I was a schoolteacher, my classes were supposed to be 45 minutes long, but if I got everything done in 30 minutes, I just quit teaching and started staring at the kids. Sometimes I'd take out a book and start to read.

"Mr. Wolfsie, what are you doing?"

"Reading a book."

"Aren't you supposed to be teaching?"

"I'm finished. That's all I want to say today about direct objects. Come to think of it, that's all I know about direct objects. Tomorrow's class is about indirect objects. I'll never get 45 minutes out of that, either. You'd better bring a book, as well."

You see, our lives are divided into neat time slots. Much of this comes from TV, which is why if we have a family conflict, my son expects it all to be solved in 30 minutes. If we can't resolve the matter in half an hour, it becomes a kind of mini series. So we argue about it for three nights. We try to start the argument on a Sunday night for two hours, but then we skip Monday night and pick it up on Tuesday. We don't settle things any better that way, but I've been told it's better for ratings.

I'm the same way on vacations. My wife wants to go away for the weekend, but I feel no obligation to stay the entire three days. Sometimes, in the middle of a piña colada on a Saturday afternoon on the beach, I'll say, "I don't want any more vacation. Let's go home." This has never worked, by the way, but it does show I had more power over my students than I have over my wife.

Well, I can stop now. I wanted to stop after those six hysterical paragraphs about clowns, so thanks for reading on even though I didn't have much else to say.

Class Act

My wife told me that my expectations were too high. She said that after 20 years you can't expect it to feel as good, to be as exciting as when you first did it as a young man. And then she hit me with the killer phrase: "And you're not as young as you used to be."

Nevertheless, I decided last week to go back to a local high school and teach English for a day. It was part of an Indianapolis initiative to get citizens into the classroom so they could experience firsthand what it's like in our city's schools.

I eagerly accepted the assignment, priding myself on having taught high school back in suburban New York City in the '70s. The art of teaching is something you never forget. "It's like riding a bike," I told myself, but then remembered that since turning 50 I've taken two serious falls from my racer, one time sustaining a minor concussion. But I still thought I could teach; I was just in search of a better analogy.

I began by reading a few excerpts from my

favorite author, E.B. White. His essay, "Death of a Pig," lent itself (at least it did in the '70s) to a discussion of various literary techniques. I began working the room Phil Donahue-style, ranting and raving about how White had taken a very common occurrence on a farm—the slaughtering of a pig for bacon—and turned it 180 degrees into a tender look at a man's love for a sick animal.

As I worked myself into a lather pontificating about the literary use of irony and the magic of White's word choices, I could tell the kids were more amused than informed by this dramatic diatribe. I think they were wondering if I had any intention of getting rid of an actual idea before the bell rang. I taught my heart out that morning. I really did. But it just wasn't the same.

I felt slightly out of place that entire day. I think that for the 10 years I taught, I managed to incrementally adjust as the years went by. Kids do change, but not as much as we think, and I managed to creep along with them over a decade, unconsciously fine tuning both technique and expectations.

Part of my personal disappointment came from two comparisons: First, my memories of 20 years ago, which have fallen victim to the halo effect—like an old relationship where you just remember the good times. And secondly, the contrast with my present occupation—media personality—which created a very unrealistic expectation of how I wanted the "audience" to react and regard me. I'm embarrassed to admit this, but probably I was a little too much into performing and not enough into teaching. And maybe, just maybe, the kids sensed it.

The students were polite and respectful. And I'm sure many of them were very bright. The problem was that I never felt I was very effective in turning up any evidence of this intelligence. I used to be so good at that.

It wasn't that I had forgotten how to teach; it was that I expected so much more out of myself. There was a part of me convinced that I could take all my expertise, all my charm and all my experience and "knock 'em dead" in sophomore English 20 years later. That just ain't the way it happened.

If someone had observed my teaching that day, I am hopeful that he would have seen the vague remnants of a past master, as I strode the aisles and preached about sentence structure and dramatic imagery. I called on students, touched shoulders to get their attention and wrestled with them to better explain their answers. But I wasn't kidding myself. I felt just a bit like the T-Rex in *Jurassic Park*, reborn temporarily to educate and entertain, but finding myself in a world in which I no longer belonged. I had great admiration for teachers that day.

Not that I had ever lost it.

Funny Business

Because of my visibility on TV and in print, my wife gets a lot of questions about how I write my humor column. Some of her favorites are:

"Is he that annoying in person?"

"Does it seem like forever that you've been married?"

"Was this an arranged marriage?"

Another common remark by people who read my column is: "Your wife certainly is funny. She says the cleverest things." This drives me up the wall because I am the one who puts the words in her mouth every week. Reading my column and then saying my wife is funny is like watching the *Flintstones* on TV and saying Barney Rubble is a great actor. The most common question is whether the stuff I write about in my newspaper columns is really true. "If it is true," people ask Mary Ellen, "why do you let him write about such personal matters? And if it's not true, why do you let him make up such baloney?" It's hard for me to win.

Most of the stuff I write about is admittedly an

exaggeration. If I said my wife went shopping and came back two days later, that is an obvious embellishment. If my wife were really gone for two days, I would call the police.

But here's the problem: I have written so many humor columns and have talked so much about comedy in my speeches that people think I am always looking for a column idea. God forbid something really tragic should actually happen..."Hello, Missing Persons Bureau? This is Dick Wolfsie. My wife has been gone for two days."

"Yes, Mr. Wolfsie, very amusing, very amusing premise, indeed. We here at Missing Persons are aware of the use of hyperbole to create a humorous and whimsical effect. By the way, we suggest three days. Those of us who have an ear for comedy know that a wife missing for two days just isn't funny enough."

"I'm not trying to be funny, officer. I believe that my friend Alan has run away with my wife."

"I think we know where you're going with this: 'And I really miss him.' Sorry, Dick, just a bit predictable. However, humor does require a twist or surprise. So the comic reversal here has potential. Just needs a little tweaking. You're on the right comedy track."

"Look, I am not writing a humor column. My wife is missing. When she last left the house, she and Alan were getting in the car with a huge suitcase."

"What a waste of potential mirth. Try saying a suitcase the size of Kokomo, or an overnight bag the size of a Pontiac. Good use of the K sound is what you're after here. By the way, scrap the name Alan. You can't picture someone named Alan. You need a Bubba or a Reginald. Think visually, for heaven's sake."

"Look, for the absolute last time, I am not writing a humor column; I am not trying to be funny. My wife has run away with my best friend, Alan, not Bubba. I do not miss him. I miss her. She has been gone two days, not three. And, I saw them leave together with a large suitcase, not a suitcase the size of Kokomo. Now, maybe I'm being a little paranoid, but doesn't that seem a little funny to you?"
"Not the way you tell it."